AC[illegible] LIBRARIANSHIP BY DESIGN

A Blended Librarian's Guide to the Tools and Techniques

Steven J. Bell
John D. Shank

American Library Association
Chicago 2007

While extensive effort has gone into ensuring the reliability of information appearing in this book, the publisher makes no warranty, express or implied, on the accuracy or reliability of the information, and does not assume and hereby disclaims any liability to any person for any loss or damage caused by errors or omissions in this publication.

Some material in this book was previously published as "Promotion through 'Teachnology': Using LTAs (Low Threshold Applications) to Collaborate with Faculty," *NetConnect* (Winter 2004): 15–16, copyright © 2004 Reed Business Information, a division of Reed Elsevier, all rights reserved; it is reprinted by permission of *Library Journal*.

The paper used in this publication meets the minimum requirements of American National Standard for Information Sciences—Permanence of Paper for Printed Library Materials, ANSI Z39.48-1992. ∞

Library of Congress Cataloging-in-Publication Data

Bell, Steven J.

Academic librarianship by design : a blended librarian's guide to the tools and techniques / Steven J. Bell, John D. Shank.

p. cm.

Includes bibliographical references (p.) and index.

ISBN-13: 978-0-8389-0939-3 (alk. paper)

1. Academic librarians. 2. Academic libraries—Relations with faculty and curriculum. 3. Instructional systems—Design. 4. Educational technology. 5. Libraries and colleges. 6. Academic librarians—Effect of technological innovations on. 7. Information literacy—Study and teaching (Higher) I. Shank, John D. II. Title.

Z682.4.C63B4 2007

027.7—dc22 2007001669

ISBN-13: 978-0-8389-0939-3

ISBN-10: 0-8389-0939-6

Printed in the United States of America

11 10 09 08 07 5 4 3 2 1

We dedicate this book to our wives, children, and colleagues whose support and patience made it possible.

Contents

Foreword

It was the best of times, it was the worst of times, . . .
—Charles Dickens, *A Tale of Two Cities*

We live in times even more paradoxical for librarians and their colleagues in higher education than Dickens described. We live in times of explosive change in the nature and quantity of information—times when many traditional fundamental skills of librarians are needed more widely and more often than ever before. We live in times of unpredictable change in the structures and strategies for managing information resources—times when many academic institutions look for options that entirely exclude traditional libraries and traditional librarians. It is painful to accept the prospect of rising costs for information management and use in education, especially when other sectors of society are alleged to have already achieved new cost efficiencies through automation. But those costs keep rising.

We are deluged with information and options. We are overwhelmed with an accelerating flood of information itself, of new forms of information, of new tools for manipulating information, of new capacities for storing and retrieving information, of new options for teaching and learning, of new ways of collaborating, and of new forms of seclusion.

We live in times of increasing need for the skills and expertise traditionally characteristic of many kinds of librarians: guiding and assisting us in taking advantage of our information environment, categorizing and storing information in ways likely to facilitate its effective retrieval, and—perhaps most valuable of all—helping novices avoid the pitfalls and find the nuggets in this ever more complex and confusing information-rich universe.

The need for universal, lifelong, hybrid professional development is growing rapidly. The technologies and strategies available to offer such professional development effectively are growing rapidly. The gap between those in need and those responsible for helping them is widening. This is as true on campus as online.

We're all tormented by the same burning question: why is it so difficult to engage the vast majority of college and university faculty members and other academics in educational activities to support their own continuing professional development?

A universally accepted definition of "information literacy" remains elusive, as does a simple set of goals and strategies for achieving them. In fact, many institutions (especially smaller private liberal arts colleges) have found it politically and culturally desirable to avoid the term entirely. However, there is a growing recognition that undergraduate students and citizens at large are increasingly seeking and using Internet-based information and resources that do not meet reasonable standards of truth, clarity, and authentication. The need to help more people—young and old—learn how to cope more effectively and efficiently with Internet-based information resources is growing much faster than the information sophistication of most computer users.

However, it is widely acknowledged among academic professionals throughout higher education—including most librarians—that librarians alone cannot meet these needs, and that new uses of information technology have yet to bring great cost savings along with great opportunities for new kinds of intellectual achievement.

Duplication of effort has long been tolerable as a by-product of support for experimentation and research. However, fiscal and political conditions at most colleges and universities are pressing administrators to find cost savings where they can. Better coordination and collaboration among diverse offices and departments within a college or university can, at least, eliminate some wasteful duplication of effort and services. More important, the authors of this book have identified areas in which collaboration that involves librarians, instructional design professionals, and representatives of some other key areas can do much more than reduce wasted effort.

As developed by Bell and Shank, the concept of the blended librarian is building new efficiencies and new accomplishments upon a foundation of new synergies—taking advantage of the very paradox that is daunting so many others. In the emerging world of blended librarianship, librarians and instructional design specialists, faculty development professionals, and technology professionals are learning from one another's expertise and developing, together, new ways of enhancing and supporting undergraduate teaching and learning—and even research. They are increasing the value of the education they help others provide.

I am impressed with the combination of imagination, insight, practical judgment, and modest optimism demonstrated by Bell and Shank's concept of blended librarianship. I am excited by what they have already achieved and by the potential for further growth demonstrated in the vitality of their work, their community, and this book.

I look forward to their continued progress, especially to what they will achieve next with the additional help of those who first discover and join the work of blended librarians through reading this book. I look forward to traveling together with them and with you on this path through and beyond paradox to new levels of insight and accomplishment.

Steven W. Gilbert
President, The TLT Group

Preface

Until recently I worked at Philadelphia University. In the universe of American higher education institutions, it is a university that can easily get lost in the crowd. Among the Ivy League institutions, the prestigious liberal arts colleges, and the nationally recognized community colleges, Philadelphia University is perhaps without great distinction. But it is an institution that has made an amazing transformation over the past decade. Where it once was primarily a textiles engineering and management institution, its curriculum today is largely shaped by design programs. The curriculum includes studies in architecture, interior design, graphic design, digital design, industrial design, instructional design, and fashion design. Many of the university's traditional programs remain, but it is clear that the study of design and its application across the disciplines has now emerged as the thread that weaves together the fabric of the institution.

This was graphically illustrated in 2004 when new banners were hung across our campus that promoted a simple but powerful concept. Each banner proclaimed "Design Matters." The new banners were raised to promote the renaissance of our institutional Design Center as a home for cultural programs that allow all to appreciate more deeply how design influences our way of living, and also to signify our institution's growing commitment to the study of a multitude of design disciplines. My passing by those banners every day, along with my own growing interest in instructional design and technology, influenced my thinking about academic librarianship and the future of this profession.

Before we began thinking about the intersection of design and librarianship, my colleague and coauthor, John Shank, and I began to explore how academic librarians might morph into a new role we call the "blended librarian." On the basis of our mutual interest in instructional technology, we believe that librarians can add to their existing skills a new skill set drawn from instructional design in order to develop a blend of traditional librarianship, information technology, and these new design possibilities. In the past two years, hundreds of librarians have shown an interest in blended librarianship by attending workshops about it or by joining the Blended Librarians Online Learning Community.

It is important to understand the core values associated with blended librarianship in order to have a deeper understanding of the references to blended librarianship, its philosophies, and its applications that we make throughout this book. At the center of blended librarianship is the conviction that we need to enhance the library's integration into the teaching and learning process (e.g., courses and curricula) occurring at our institutions. The blended librarian believes that the best way to achieve this is by applying design thinking to the development and enhancement of library services. This involves utilizing both existing and emerging instructional technologies (e.g., course/learning management systems, podcasts, blogs, digital learning materials, etc.) in the process. Additionally, we need to partner and form learning communities with our faculty, instructional designers and technologists, and other staff as well as with these professionals at other institutions to successfully design and use instructional technologies and ultimately enhance the library services and products offered to our patrons.

As its title suggests, this book is about more than blended librarianship. It is about design. But design takes many forms and shapes and infiltrates itself into many professions. We use the blended librarian concept to create a framework for better understanding how an academic librarian can develop a design philosophy that he or she will use to guide the development of instructional products. To do this, each chapter follows a format that we believe will encourage constructive learning by the reader. Each chapter begins with a set of learning objectives. These are followed by a brief introduction to the content of the chapter. Several of the chapters help the reader connect past experience with new material in the chapter by presenting scenarios or examples that identify how these concepts and ideas could play a role in changing the profession in the future. The main content of the chapter is followed, when appropriate, by case studies or profiles to further illustrate the concepts and principles presented in that chapter. Chapters conclude with topics for further discussion and additional resources.

The book is organized into three core themes. The first theme, covered in chapters 1–4, introduces the reader to blended librarianship and design thinking and the connection between them. At this point, let's just say that blended librarianship is a practitioner's framework for incorporating design thinking into our practice, and that design thinking is an expression of this new persona. The outcome of bringing the two together is to use creative and thoughtful processes to innovate new learning products or services or to improve our existing ones. Chapter 2 delves further into design thinking, while chapters 3 and 4 respectively explore instructional design and using it to create better connections with faculty that lead to collaboration.

The second theme, covered in chapters 5–7, lays out eminently practical manifestations of blended librarianship and design thinking. It is primarily in these chapters that the tools and techniques mentioned in the book's subtitle are further discussed.

The third theme, covered in chapters 8 and 9, explores how academic librarians can rethink their own roles and the repositioning of their libraries in communities of colleagues with similar ambitions, and how technology will play a prominent role in bringing about the evolution of the blended librarian.

Our intention in this book is to engage and encourage the reader to visit and join the Blended Librarians Online Learning Community and actively contribute to the development of blended librarianship. This will also allow readers to further engage with colleagues who have read the book and wish to discuss it in the online community.

We think the timing for the ideas we present in this book is critical because academic librarianship is being challenged in ways not imaginable even a decade ago, and in an age of rapid technological advances it is likely our professional world will change even more dramatically in the next five years. We are moving into a new information environment that is being shaped by two polar opposites, simplicity and complexity. While our academic libraries are inherently complex owing to their scale and the complexity of information they harbor, the information needs, expectations, and search behaviors of most of our users are influenced by the relative simplicity of popular search engines and e-commerce sites. One of our challenges is to use the power of design to create a library user experience that is situational in nature, so that it can respond at the appropriate level at which the user wants to interact with the library. To do otherwise may only hasten the growing marginalization of the academic library.

The idea of design thinking is something we return to throughout this book. We think this book will add a valuable perspective to the existing literature about the academic library profession. However, it is quite different from many of the texts about academic librarianship that have preceded it. We recognize that there are already some useful texts for those who want to know what academic librarianship is about, how it fits into the greater scheme of the higher education enterprise, and what the basic functionalities of the academic library and its librarians are. Instead, we focus on how a design philosophy, something we refer to as "design thinking," can inform our practice and serve as a guide to thoughtful thinking and processes as we perform the many different functions that contribute to academic librarianship.

Steven Bell

Acknowledgments

We would like to acknowledge the contributions of our colleagues who provided profiles and case studies for the book. We greatly appreciate the time and effort they put into their contributions. We wish to acknowledge the LearningTimes Network for its support of the Blended Librarians Online Learning Community since 2004. Special thanks go to Hope Kandel of the LearningTimes Network for all the help she has provided in supporting blended librarian programming. We would also like to thank our friends and colleagues who have provided support to the Blended Librarians Online Learning Community: Lisa Allen, Karen Wetzel, and Lauren Pressley. And finally, we wish to acknowledge the longtime support of Steve Gilbert, president of the TLT Group, for believing in our ideas and helping us to make blended librarianship more than just an idea. Thanks to all of you.

1 Where It All Begins
Blended Librarianship

The future of the library is that there is no library; the functions that the library performs have been blown up and are scattered throughout the universe. —Leigh Watson Healy, Outsell, Inc.

OBJECTIVES

1. Provide some historical context to blended librarianship; describe its origins and how it developed.
2. Connect the concept of blended librarianship to the practice of academic librarianship.
3. Describe how blended librarianship can facilitate the application of design thinking to professional practice.
4. Provide profiles of different blended librarians to illustrate the type of work they perform.

RETHINKING YOUR ROLE AS AN ACADEMIC LIBRARIAN

Perhaps you were drawn to this book by the title. What does design have to do with the practice of academic librarianship? Perhaps you heard a reference to the Blended Librarians Online Learning Community or encountered a colleague who mentioned being a blended librarian and you wanted to investigate further. What does it mean to be a blended librarian? Perhaps the word *design* resonated with you because you've encountered other references to the importance of design, and you thought it was time to learn how to incorporate design thinking into your practice. The two concepts, design and academic librarianship, are connected, and you will learn how and in what ways throughout this book.

In brief, the connection is instructional design. Academic librarians, at the core of their profession, are educators. Whether they are employed in public or technical service areas, the work of academic librarians is directed to helping students and faculty achieve academic success. Instructional design is a set of skills that are used by many educators to create products that enable people to learn more effectively. Instructional design can help us make academic success possible by improving our approach to the construction and implementation of new library services and resources. Along the way, another powerful influence in the development of our ideas and practices is design thinking.

Our goal is simply to present ideas, tools, and techniques to our colleagues and then allow them to determine for themselves if these methods hold promise. For us, being blended librarians means exploring new ways of improving services to our faculty colleagues and students. Our intention is always to share our thoughts and strategies about how we might best accomplish this and never crosses over into fervent evangelism to convince academic librarians that they need to be like us. We hope that this book offers the information you need to make the determination for yourself, or that you can make use of the concepts and practices to develop something new and different for yourself or the profession. In doing so, we anticipate that you will have an opportunity to rethink your role as an academic librarian.

ARE YOU A BLENDED LIBRARIAN?

Do you know an instructional designer or instructional technologist? The odds are good that your academic institution employs one or more individuals in either or both of these positions. These positions might be located in academic computing, information technology, the learning center, or quite possibly the academic library. Just exactly what do they do, and how do these two roles differ? Instructional technology typically refers to the hardware, software, and systems created specifically for or adapted to an educational purpose; a chalkboard, an iPod, a clicker (personal response system), and a simulation game are all instructional technologies because they can be used to transmit information from a source to a receiver and aid in the development of learned skills. Instructional technologists work with faculty to match the appropriate technologies to teaching and assist faculty in the effective use of technologies for teaching. For example, at many higher education institutions, instructional technologists support the faculty's use of courseware management systems. Many faculty initially use courseware to electronically disseminate their traditional materials. How do faculty go from using courseware simply to store their syllabus and lecture slides to using it to engage students in the learning process? That's where instructional technologists do their work. They show faculty how to use courseware tools such as discussion boards, group activities, feedback quizzes, and other integrated learning tools to achieve better pedagogy through technology. Instructional technologists are experts in understanding how to use technology tools to enhance the teaching and learning process.

Instructional design is the systematic creation of an educational experience that will help students achieve a specified set of learning outcomes. An instructional designer, knowing the learning theory and strategies to ensure quality instruction, takes an instructional problem and goes through an analysis that has several well-defined steps, and the outcome is a learning activity or instructional product (DeBlois 2005). Instructional designers are frequently called on to help faculty develop new programs or courses from scratch. Faculty are the subject matter experts, but the instructional designer is the expert at organizing the curriculum in a way that achieves the best pedagogical outcomes. Instructional technologists work almost exclusively with technology solutions or advise faculty when technology may not be the solution. By contrast, instructional designers focus on the pedagogy rather than the technology. Their focus is on identifying learning gaps, understanding the problems that stand between learners and what they need to master, and identifying the products or strategies that will enable students to achieve academic success. In many cases, this means helping faculty with pedagogical methods that involve no technology at all.

Have you ever helped a faculty member learn how to use a library database? How about integrating links to library resources into a course management system (courseware) site? Have you ever done a survey to determine how to best meet the information needs of a set of students and then developed a tutorial to resolve that information need? At one time or another, most academic librarians have likely accomplished a number of tasks that could fit into instructional design or instructional technology without even knowing it. In fact, of the many kinds of designers in different professions, academic librarians may identify most closely with instructional designers or instructional technologists.

This meshing of skill sets is in fact what blended librarianship is all about. The blended librarian retains the traditional values of academic librarianship but brings new tools—instructional design and technology skills—into the mix. How he or she accomplishes this—through intentionality and planning, in other words, *by design*—is the focus of this book. Our close study of instructional design and technology, along with collaborations with our colleagues in this field, makes clear that design thinking is critical to these professions. An appropriate and effective instructional product, as well as support to those who use instructional technologies, is the outcome of a design process. In this chapter we will focus on blended librarianship and will share profiles of individuals who serve as models of blended librarians. Blended librarianship is relatively new; no formal association governs it, nor do any standards exist to signify when it is achieved. While we can point to more specific characteristics and overarching principles, providing models is an effective method to describe what blended librarians do, what sets them apart from regular librarians, and how they apply design thinking in their work.

A BRIEF HISTORY

The roots of blended librarianship may be found in a paragraph of an article that Steven Bell published in *Portal: Libraries and the Academy* in 2003. In the article, "A Passion for Academic Librarianship: Find It, Keep It, Sustain It," Bell wrote:

> Librarians will need more than technology savvy to achieve true integration into the teaching and learning process. Our colleagues in information technology and instructional technology are endowed with technology skills as well. How do we differentiate ourselves in this arena? We can pursue a new role, one I refer to as the "Blended Librarian." The Blended Librarian first combines the traditional aspects of librarianship with the technology skills of an information technologist, someone skilled with software and hardware. Many librarians already demonstrate sound technology skills of this type. To this mix the Blended Librarian adds the instructional or educational technologist's skills for curriculum design, and the application of technology for student-centered learning. Few librarians have instructional technology skills. Library science curricula need re-structuring that adds some pedagogical foundation to the academic librarian's professional education. The Blended Librarian is the academic professional who offers the best combination of skills and services to help faculty apply technology for enhanced teaching and learning. (Bell 2003)

It was a chance meeting that took an idea from this article and turned it into something concrete. The following is a brief timeline of the development of the Blended Librarians Online Learning Community.

October 2003

This book's two authors, Steven Bell and John Shank, met at a regional teaching and learning conference when they sat next to each other at a presentation. As they got to talking, Bell was interested to hear that Shank held a position at his campus that involved both reference librarianship and instructional design. The conversation turned to the blended librarian concept, and it occurred to both that Shank's position was a potential model. The two decided to give the idea further study and to take that single paragraph and develop it into a more detailed description of what exactly blended librarianship would entail.

November 2003

Bell and Shank developed a skeletal framework for their ideas and considered how they might introduce it to other academic librarians. When it was time to share the basic concept of blended librarianship with others to get feedback, Bell decided to present the idea to Steve Gilbert, president of the Teaching, Learning, and Technology (TLT) Group. At that time the blended librarianship idea was only in the formative stage. Bell explained it as a way of introducing more librarians to the work that instructional designers and technologists were doing at academic institutions. He suggested to Gilbert that this could be a way of encouraging more academic librarians to collaborate with designers, technologists, and faculty. While Gilbert was initially curious about (and possibly even skeptical of) the idea, he provided some valuable insights into how the blended librarianship concept could provide support for librarians in the area of information literacy. Gilbert agreed to think more about the concept and develop additional suggestions for Bell and Shank. Gilbert came back with a suggestion that became a watershed in the future development of the blended librarian. He thought that an online workshop on blended librarianship and information literacy could be of interest to academic librarians, faculty, and other academic support professionals. He asked Bell and Shank to develop a workshop that could be presented through the TLT Group's collaborative workshop series with the Association of College and Research Libraries (ACRL). They agreed to do so, and the workshop was scheduled for April 2004.

April 2004

Bell and Shank decided that they needed to articulate their ideas about blended librarianship in conjunction with the workshop. That document was referred to as the Blended Librarians Manifesto. It identified the rationale for blended librarianship, the principles upon which it was based, and the ways in which it might be practically integrated by academic librarians. The manifesto was then rewritten for publication in *College and Research Libraries News* (Bell and Shank 2004). Conducting the TLT Group/ACRL online workshop also led to another significant development in blended librarianship. Bell and Shank had decided from the start that they wanted their concept to be more than just an article published in a journal or a onetime workshop. What they really wanted was to create a way to give library practitioners an opportunity to learn about blended librarianship, and to develop the instructional design and technology skills that could contribute to the growth of blended librarianship within the profession. Based on Shank's experience with presenting at an online library conference sponsored by the LearningTimes Network and the fact that LearningTimes hosted the TLT Group's online workshops, Bell and Shank got in touch with Hope Kandel, a production specialist at the network. After the workshop, Bell and Shank realized that the LearningTimes Network could be the ideal setting for a virtual learning community for blended librarians.

May 2004

Bell and Shank presented to Kandel their ideas for developing an online community for blended librarians. They wanted to encourage librarians to join in online discussions about teaching and learning skills, and to share useful articles about instructional design and technology, and they wanted to host webcasts that would feature experts and issues related to the field of instructional design and technology. The online community would be a place to learn about and share information for the advancement of blended librarianship. With support from the LearningTimes Network, Bell and Shank were able to create the Blended Librarians Online Learning Community in 2004. After two years and several more TLT Group/ACRL workshops, face-to-face workshops around the country, multiple webcasts, and discussion board postings, the Blended Librarians Online Learning Community is now a thriving enterprise with well over 2,000 members. Along with the blended librarians website at http://blendedlibrarian.org, there are now excellent opportunities for academic librarians to learn about blended librarianship and to integrate instructional design and technology skills into their traditional skill set. In the future, blended librarians will be able to further explore academic librarianship by design as these principles become further integrated into blended librarianship.

BLENDED LIBRARIANS MANIFESTO

This chapter began with a quote from Leigh Watson Healy of Outsell, Inc., from several years ago. Healy's assertion that "the future of the library is that there is no library" resonated strongly with us because an initial impetus for our thinking about blended librarianship was the observation that academic librarianship was at a critical professional juncture. We saw a growing ambiguity about the role of the academic librarian in the future academic enterprise. In response to what we viewed as forces converging to marginalize the academic librarian, we wrote our initial treatise on blended librarianship and titled it the Blended Librarians Manifesto because it put forth the issues confronting academic librarianship and the ways in which members of the profession could respond. First, the manifesto identified a set of observations about the current information landscape. These observations reflected on a number of trends that were already contributing or had the potential to contribute to the marginalization of academic librarianship:

Ubiquitous courseware systems allow faculty to create information silos that serve as gateways to all course-related information, including research sources that may or may not include the campus library.

Textbook publishers are moving to incorporate traditional library database content into websites that are companion tools for students as they use the text.

Google and other search engines! Need more be said?

A radical transformation in scholarly publishing is creating new avenues by which scholars can make their research available, potentially heralding the demise of traditional journals upon which our collections are based and throwing into question whether libraries will continue to serve as the primary conduit for scholarly literature.

Personalized subscription databases are now being marketed to individuals as an alternative to existing libraries. Questia has struggled to make this concept viable, but it's only a matter of time until a better model evolves.

"Book searching" available through Amazon.com and Google, despite its inadequacies, became immensely popular almost immediately, has received tremendous media adulation, and makes libraries, despite our technology, seem old and shopworn. Now Google is migrating all types of traditional library content, including scholarly and popular articles, into its search engine.

The "Googlization" phenomenon, in which librarians and database producers are driving a movement to make our systems emulate Google, makes us look desperate and fearful that our days of teaching end users to develop efficient research skills are over.

These and other trends suggested that if the future is one in which there is no library—or at least not the library that exists as our traditional communal paradigm of what an academic library is supposed to be—then our profession was in the perfect position to transform the academic library and the role of the academic librarian. The manifesto states:

> It is imperative and no exaggeration to claim that the future of academic librarianship depends on our collective ability to integrate services and practices into the teaching and learning process. While the evolution of information literacy is a positive sign, the academic librarian is still largely tangential to what happens in or beyond the classroom. Strategies, techniques and skills are needed that can allow all academic librarians, from every sector of the library organization, to proactively advance their integration into the teaching and learning process. The framework

> envisioned depends largely upon the ability to collaborate with faculty, but also other campus information and instructional technologists. This framework is best expressed as the "blended librarian."

Although the premise of the blended librarian was more theory than practice at this early stage, a simple definition evolved:

> A Blended Librarian is an academic librarian who combines the traditional skill set of librarianship with the information technologist's hardware/software skills, and the instructional or educational designer's ability to apply technology appropriately in the teaching-learning process.

To expand further on the definition, we identified six principles for blended librarianship:

Taking a leadership position as campus innovators and change agents to successfully deliver library services in today's "information society"

Committing to developing campuswide information literacy initiatives on our campuses to facilitate our ongoing involvement in the teaching and learning process

Designing instructional and educational programs and classes to assist patrons in using library services and learning information literacy that are absolutely essential to gaining the necessary skills (trade) and knowledge (profession) for lifelong success

Collaborating and engaging in dialogue with instructional technologists and designers, which is vital to the development of programs, services, and resources needed to facilitate the instructional mission of academic libraries

Implementing adaptive, creative, proactive, and innovative change in library instruction, which can be enhanced by communicating and collaborating with newly created instructional technology/design librarians and existing instructional designers and technologists

Transforming our relationship with faculty to emphasize our ability to assist them with integrating information technology and library resources into courses, but adding to that traditional role a new capacity to collaborate on enhancing student learning and outcome assessment in the area of information access, retrieval, and integration

As originally perceived, blended librarianship would reverse the marginalization of academic librarianship by making it more central to what happens in learning spaces, both physical and virtual. The goal was never to eliminate other information competitors from those same learning spaces or to brainwash students to use only the academic library's information resources. Even in the unlikely event this could be accomplished, the real goal was simply to integrate the academic library into the teaching and learning process in a way that would enable faculty and students to achieve better balance in their research and use whatever tools were most appropriate for that research, whether these tools were coming from the library or otherwise. Through faculty collaboration, by providing faculty and students with digital learning materials to support their understanding and use of the library's resources, and by applying design thinking to the resolution of barriers to their goals, we believe blended librarianship can help other academic librarians to connect more effectively with faculty and students seeking information. Although we did not realize it at the time, many of the attributes of blended librarianship were forms of academic librarianship by design.

BLENDED LIBRARIANSHIP: A FRAMEWORK FOR ACADEMIC LIBRARIANSHIP BY DESIGN

Tim Brown, CEO and president of IDEO, says that design thinking is "inherently a prototyping process." Designers use prototypes to create a rough version of a product, system, or service, and they do so because it can be done quickly and at lower cost. The goal is not to create a finished product quickly. The goal is to use the prototype to elicit feedback that helps to resolve a problem. Design thinking is about making things better and creating a catalyst for innovation (Brown 2005). Design thinking is also a hallmark of academic librarianship by design. Blended librarianship itself is largely a product of design thinking. It was developed quickly, primarily in order to create a workshop from rough ideas that were still going through the formative process. The early version of blended librarianship was a prototype, and through feedback from participants, it was continually modified as it grew. According to Brown, design thinking is ideally suited to endeavors such as this that require moving from concepts to real, tangible outcomes. As it matures, blended librarianship will better serve as a personal and practical framework that individual librarians can use to integrate academic librarianship by design into their skill set and knowledge.

A changing academic library environment requires librarians who can innovate, discover, and implement new services. Tim Brown talks about individuals who are inquisitive about the world and are willing to try to integrate the skills of what others do into their own work. He calls them "T-shaped people." They have a principal skill (the vertical leg of the T), but they are so empathetic, or understanding of the users' needs or situation, that they can branch out into other skills (the top of the T) and do them as well. Blended librarians are T-shaped people. In searching for ways to improve their ability to support and connect with faculty, in striving to improve the quality of their own instruction, and in reaching out to students by designing ways of integrating the library into their learning spaces, blended librarians have added instructional design and technology skills on top of their traditional library skills. Having integrated these skills, the blended librarian is well adapted to practice academic librarianship by design.

Another useful perspective on the blended librarian comes from Richard Farson. He is the founding dean of the School of Design at the California Institute of the Arts and a thirty-year member of the Board of Directors of the International Design Conference, and he writes about the intersection between design and management. Farson talks about social architects. Architects are designers. Social architects are also designers, but they design organizational change. They ask how a change in the arrangement or structure of a place or process can create more efficiency or innovation. A social architect might ask, "How can I organize our team so workflow is aligned with stated goals?" (Farson 2005). Social architects seek to create thoughtful, purposeful change. Blended librarians seek to create similar change to better integrate the academic library into the learning process at an academic institution. Like social architects who ask how to create more efficient teams, blended librarians attempt to design both learning products and systems that allow faculty to make use of the library's resources in ways that achieve better connections with learners. Blended librarians use technology tools and techniques to create the structures that support student learning in all possible campus spaces, physical and virtual.

PROFILES OF BLENDED LIBRARIANS

Now that you have a better understanding of how blended librarianship was created, how it evolved, and how it connects to our concept of academic librarianship by design, this is a good time to learn more about what some blended librarians do and how they became blended. In addition to providing profiles for ourselves, we asked several of our blended librarianship colleagues to share their own profiles. Through these profiles we hope to provide a better, more concrete understanding of what blended librarians do, what they are and are not, and how one develops the appropriate skill set.

Steven Bell, Associate University Librarian for Research and Instructional Services

I've been a librarian just shy of thirty years. It is the only profession I've practiced. For the vast majority of my career I had no knowledge of instructional design or technology. My earliest exposure to some basic instructional technology applications came during the late 1990s. While working as a board member of a local academic library organization, I met John Shank's predecessor at the Berks campus of Penn State University. She was doing instructional design work, mostly helping faculty develop websites and some basic multimedia materials. I was impressed by her work, but more so by her outlook on how faculty could integrate technology in their courses. At this time I was early in my career at Philadelphia University as the director of the library and just getting to know the curriculum. Based on my prior exposure to instructional design, I was most interested in the university's Instructional Design and Technology program. Initially, I thought that coursework in instructional design and technology would strengthen my knowledge of pedagogy and learning, disciplines in which I had no formal education. In my role as director of the library at Philadelphia University, I also had more responsibility for leading the institution's effort to expand the use of technology for teaching and learning, and a better understanding of teaching technology would enable me to provide better leadership.

I was correct, but I didn't realize there is much more to instructional design and technology than pedagogy. Although I was learning some material on my own, it began to influence my thinking about blended librarianship. I realized I could do more than just think about how adding instructional technology skills to what I already knew would improve me as a librarian. I realized I could take a variety of courses to gain a more concrete understanding of these different skills. And that's what I did, setting out on the path to developing my skills as a blended librarian. In particular, I chose to earn a Pennsylvania Instructional Technology Specialist certificate. It is a post-master's program that requires six core courses in instructional design and technology. I've taken the foundation courses, all of which have tremendously increased my knowledge of instructional technologies and their sensible use for educational applications. It's given me a greater appreciation of what I can accomplish as a blended librarian.

Sean Cordes, Instructional Technology Librarian, Iowa State University

Having started my academic career in the fields of psychology and English at the University of Missouri, it was some years before I found my way to the world of libraries. Nonetheless, my understanding of the power to use technology to organize and teach information skills began to bloom. Then, as a graduate student in educational technology and library science, the technical and philosophical foundation of my career took shape; database management and web design classes wove together with library courses covering reference, collection development, and cataloging. Professionally, I began a position on Project WhistleStop, an educational web project at the Harry S. Truman Library and Museum. I also became the webmaster of several large academic websites at the University of Missouri, including the Office of Minority Affairs, the Office of the ADA Coordinator, and others.

In 2002 my library experience began as manager of a project at the Missouri Department of Transportation. We cataloged over 5,000 records using laptops from distributed points and set up circulation and virtual reference services. This experience melded my instructional technology skills with a library systems setting. The stage for my blended career was set.

Degrees in hand, I began my role as the instructional technology librarian at Iowa State University in 2004. When the position was created, it was not clear whether it would reside in the Reference or the Information Technology Department. Ultimately, I found a home in Reference and Instruction. From this early dualism, I began to realize the scope of the blended role. Library instruction could be the key to providing lifelong information skills for student learners. Learning technology was a ticket to the ride. But I was unsure how librarianship could forge the bond between these areas. It was through my early professional experience that the role of librarianship in the equation became clear.

Currently my duties and responsibilities are "to provide leadership in developing the effective use of technology throughout the library and overall campus instruction program." Effective librarianship cannot occur in a vacuum. To broaden the impact of librarianship on our campus I work closely with campus instructional technology, central computing, teaching faculty, and others critical to the best practice of technology in the learning process. Furthermore, I represent the library in campus groups like the Teaching and Learning Circle and the Faculty Senate IT Committee. On my own initiative, I developed an educational technology event series that creates a common ground in the library for sharing and dialoguing about experiences related to technology in the teaching and learning process.

Efforts like these help generate an impression of the library as a technology leader and librarians as champions for the transfer of information service and learning technology across the university mission. In this way I am helping to blend librarianship, technology, and teaching in a way that can lead libraries and academia into a positive future.

Christine Herz, Reference Librarian, Gloucester County College

In 2001 a desire to do more teaching led me from law libraries to an academic library at a community college. At the Jenkins Public Law Library in Philadelphia, where I was working at the time, I had been developing courses to teach attorneys how to search and find legal information on the Internet. In this new role as a teacher and trainer charged with writing and organizing the accompanying course materials, I felt stretched in my capacity as an educator. Legal information and access to county and local government data was a gap that the Internet was just beginning to fill. Our legal clientele was in need of more opportunities to learn how to navigate the new digital territory.

As our course offerings at the Jenkins Law Library expanded, I realized there was much I needed to learn in order to enhance my skills as an educator. I eagerly took advantage of the community of librarians and information professionals from the Greater Philadelphia Law Library Association (GPLLA) and the Philadelphia Chapter of the Special Libraries Association. In fact, I ended up cochairing the Internet Trainers Group as the result of a "brown-bag lunch" meeting of GPLLA librarians. The committee met monthly and discussed teaching, tips, and technology tools. One of the presenters was the then-director of the Instructional Design and Technology master's program at Philadelphia University. Along with a graduate student, the director gave a sample of the capstone projects from students enrolled in the program. I was impressed with the depth of the design and development and the final products created. The following autumn, I enrolled in the program.

As an Internet teacher and trainer in the legal profession, I never intended to leave for a reference post at a community college—but I did. Fortuitously, I found that the course assignments and projects in the Instructional Design and Technology program integrated well with my job responsibilities. For example, a collaborative webquest assignment fit into information literacy initiatives I was developing, and online courses in the Philadelphia University program taught me the benefits of online learning. Thus I was prepared to teach in a blended environment, interacting with students both face-to-face and online. A year later I designed and taught a class, "Computerized Legal Research," for paralegals. While in school, I worked as co-instructional designer on our final capstone project team. We did a "needs analysis" of the learning "gap," analyzed the data, created learning modules based on that analysis, and, to engage the students, wrote quiz questions and sought feedback to assess their learning. After two semesters, the final product became a polished, interactive, and exciting learning piece.

As the reference librarian and person responsible for our information literacy outreach, the knowledge and skills I acquired through the instructional design program are still essential. They allow me to plan effective instructional sessions or classes, write appropriate course materials and handouts, and create interactive web demonstrations and simulations. While software and technology constantly change, I realized that sound instructional design theory and concepts do not, and that is what empowers me in my blended librarian role.

Lauren Pressley, Microtext Assistant, Wake Forest University; Library Student, University of North Carolina at Greensboro

I did not go to college to become a librarian, but soon after I graduated I realized I should become one. After graduation I obtained a job as the microtext assistant at Wake Forest University. The environment, the day-to-day work, and supportive colleagues helped me recognize that I should go to library school and become a librarian.

About the time I joined the Wake Forest staff, the campus community began showing increasing interest in a one-credit-hour information literacy class. Wake Forest also places a high value on technology by positioning itself as a "ThinkPad campus," where every student has a ThinkPad laptop. Starting out at a university that valued library instruction and technology focused me on a "blended librarian" mind-set.

Early in my position, I developed a training program for the twenty-five student employees in the Microtext and Government Documents Departments of my library. Part of this project involved creating a student training wiki as an asynchronous tool that could act as both a repository and an instructional device. This entry-level experience showed me that I would need to have a better background in educational techniques and technology to play an effective role in libraries.

A few months into the job, I also realized that to do everything I wanted to do in libraries I would need to go to library school. I enrolled at the University of North Carolina at Greensboro and have focused my studies on instructional design and emerging technologies. To flesh out the traditional MLIS curriculum, I have taken courses in instructional design and library instruction and electives from the Curriculum and Instruction Department.

As I have progressed toward the MLIS degree, my colleagues have supported my professional growth by allowing me to help with reference and to coteach information literacy classes. This experience has allowed me to incorporate skills from both the traditional classes of the MLIS program and those gleaned from the Curriculum and Instruction Department classes. I also work on increasing my blended skill set through a practicum designing appropriate learning objects for library instruction. The practicum aims to develop short, modular Flash "games" that teach basic information-searching concepts. This practicum draws on skill sets in librarianship, instructional design, and technology.

I still have a year left in my program, but I can already tell that my instruction and technology backgrounds help in my current job, and once I find a position as a librarian, they will benefit my library as well. I fully believe that the skill set that blended librarians bring to the table will only become more important as librarians continue to incorporate instructional design principles and educational technology into the library experience for our users.

John Shank, Assistant Instructional Design Librarian and Director of the Center for Learning Technologies, Penn State University, Berks Campus

Like many librarians, I did not go to college to become a librarian. The idea of becoming a librarian did not occur to me until several years after I graduated from college, but the seed was planted while I attended Earlham College. This environment provided me with an exceptional firsthand experience of how effective library instruction programs can be when they are successfully integrated into both the general curriculum and individual courses. I left Earlham with strong information literacy skills that I did not fully appreciate until I began my graduate studies at Drexel University. While pursuing my master's degree in library science, I took the course Introduction to Information Systems Analysis. This course introduced me to the concepts of systems analysis and design. I did not have a chance to fully begin to apply my design skills until I began working at Bryn Mawr College as a technology specialist in 2000. This grant-funded position was new and unique because it was shared between the library and the computing center. The position was part of an initiative to "strengthen the teaching/learning environment and deepen cooperation and collaboration among faculty, librarians, computing personnel, and instructional support staffs." While a large part of my responsibilities was to establish the library's electronic reserves system, it was also at this time that I was appointed to the college's instructional technology team. I began to delve more fully into instructional system design and instructional technology while serving as a member of this team.

The culmination of my skills, knowledge, and interests came about when I was hired by the Penn State University Libraries in 2001 to be the instructional design librarian at the Berks campus. At the time I was hired I was one of the first in the country to hold such a position. Today I find myself among a small (approximately two dozen) but growing number of instructional design librarians in the United States. Most significantly, I am the only instructional design librarian whose responsibilities encompass more than providing instructional design support for just the library.

At Penn State Berks, my duties and responsibilities are to support all of the College's faculty and curricula. To best accomplish this, I was appointed head of the College's Instructional Design Services in 2002. In the summer of 2004, I was named director of the College's Center for Learning Technologies (CLT). The blending of my positions as instructional design librarian and as director of the CLT enables me to take a leadership role on campus. Blending the knowledge and skills of the two professions allows me to more effectively identify, design, develop, and assess appropriate instructional technologies that faculty can use to enhance the quality of the student-centered learning environment. This position has allowed me to share my understanding of how important the library is to the instructional mission of universities and colleges.

Kathryn G. Shaughnessy, Instructional Services Librarian, St. John's University Library

I grew up in libraries. Every summer I was conscripted to work in my mother's high school library. When I wasn't reading the books that I was supposed to be processing, I inked filmstrips, created signage, and even typed catalog cards. We were both glad to see the advent of personal computers in the early 1980s and the attendant time-saving processes they ushered in, but I also got hooked on the language and structure behind computers—especially the logical structure behind programming and the myriad ways to organize and cross-reference data. My fascination with the potential of computers led to a permanent subtrend in all my subsequent jobs: I was the one in the department who liked to figure out the recently purchased, but as yet unimplemented, software program. In college I majored in philosophy with a minor in MIS, and I worked in libraries to pay for my undergraduate and graduate degrees and the subsequent dissertation years. I could see that the teaching and learning that were taking place in my philosophy classroom were increasingly overlapping with the teaching and learning that were taking place in the library, and that technology was clearly facilitating this pedagogical overlap in unprecedented ways.

After getting an MLS in academic librarianship, I was hired as faculty for an instructional services librarian position at St. John's University in New York. They were looking for someone who had college-level teaching experience, a knowledge of information resources, and a facility with emerging-technology applications in higher education. The job is part bricks-and-mortar teaching, part remote instruction, and part outreach to all faculty, with the ultimate goal of creating real collaborative partnerships that promote information fluency across all levels of scholarship on campus.

The latter part of the job has included working with the university's Center for Teaching and Learning and the university's Title III project team to help create assignments that further information literacy and critical thinking goals, and to help faculty in using existing or emerging library resources that faculty may or may not know about. Recent projects include training faculty to set up profiles that enable research to go to them through RSS and e-mail alerts from the OPAC and databases. My job also includes modeling the use of new technologies for faculty in ways that might help meet their pedagogical goals; to this end, I have worked with the Department of Library and Information Science to demonstrate the instructional uses of podcasts, blogs, wikis, social tagging, and Skype, the latter of which has enabled me to be a guest lecturer in online classes or a remote lecturer in an on-campus class when I am on a different campus.

Eileen Stec, Instruction and Outreach Librarian, Rutgers, State University of New Jersey

I consider myself both a blended and a reflective librarian. Like many librarians, I began my professional life in another field—social work. Psychiatric social work requires the practitioner to focus, observe, and develop a working diagnosis and to adapt a treatment plan to each group or individual under her care. Reflection became second nature to me and in librarianship manifested itself as assessment. In the public library it was natural to observe the learning difficulties of patrons. Many people lack a knowledge of call number systems and struggle with technology. My first "aha!" moment occurred when I was a medical librarian. At the time, many medical students were just learning how to use electronic indexes. I would dutifully draw Venn diagrams explaining how combining terms worked. Fully one-third of the students looked lost when I used this teaching approach. Certainly this user population had the intelligence to grasp the concept of combining terms, so the fault must lie with my pedagogy.

I made it my business to learn how people learn. I observed classes taught by a colleague with an undergraduate education degree and discussed my concerns with her. Betty Warner's mentoring took me to the next step. I recognized my own preferred learning style. To avoid learning method bias in my teaching, I began using multimedia technology to effectively accommodate learning styles different from my own.

I enrolled in a graduate Instructional Design program at Philadelphia University. The program was profiled by Joyce Valenza (a high school media specialist) in her *Philadelphia Inquirer* newspaper column. Technology is infused in every theory course, and pedagogy is either taught or reinforced in technology courses. My program instructors were either K–12 educators or from the technology industry. As a matter of integrity, I enrolled in one fully online distance learning course;

how can one teach what one has not experienced? My most profound experience was in marshaling the bravery to use the teaching exercises I had experienced in class. Would a constructivist teaching approach be as effective for my students as it had been for me? In a word, yes. Since then, I have used a hybrid learning approach, utilizing face-to-face instruction exercises and creating multimedia discovery learning tools. Two of my tutorials are used nationally at higher education institutions.

One of my most gratifying accomplishments is collaborating with Jana Varlejs of Rutgers University and the graduate Library Studies students from her User Instruction course. I designed a library instruction curriculum as a practicum for the graduate students, who in turn taught the curriculum to the undergraduate students enrolled in my college's mission course. In six years collaborating with the User Instruction course, over sixty graduate students gained teaching skills and experience. Six of these graduate students volunteered or were employed part-time by the Rutgers University Libraries as library instructors, alleviating the shortage of teaching librarians. As a result of my efforts with the User Instruction students, over 200 undergraduate bibliographic instruction classes have been taught, gaining over 4,700 more undergraduate student instruction contacts than were possible with the available full-time librarians.

CONCLUSION

We hope this chapter has provided greater insight into blended librarianship. As we have explored this concept and continue to ground it in practice, we realize that it can sometimes be misunderstood. Most frequently, we find that librarians equate multitasking with being blended. That is, for the uninitiated, being blended means wearing many hats in the workplace. There are few librarians who don't juggle many jobs, each of which can include some mix of traditional library skills, such as reference, and information technology, such as using specialized computer software. But multitasking is not synonymous with blended librarianship. It is about more than taking care of a number of different responsibilities in the library. It's about integrating new skill sets from instructional design and technology into one's practice and using those skills to better integrate the library into the teaching and learning process. Bear in mind that blended librarianship is not just a theory or words on paper. It is embodied in the activities at the Blended Librarians Online Learning Community, as that community provides a virtual space to learn more about these skills from those who practice them.

TOPICS FOR FURTHER DISCUSSION

Where in your present library position do you see opportunities for blending instructional design and technology skills? How about your coworkers?

Does your institution hire instructional designers or instructional technologists? If so, what is your relationship with them? Is there ongoing collaboration between the librarians and the instructional designers and technologists? If so, what can you learn from them about integrating technology into library services? If not, how can you begin a dialogue?

In your current position at your library, where do you see opportunities to work more closely with faculty to help them learn how to more effectively use library technologies? What is one technology you would feel comfortable teaching faculty how to use?

ADDITIONAL RESOURCE

For more information on blended librarians, visit the blended librarians website at http://blendedlibrarian.org. The site contains information on how to join the Blended Librarians Online Learning Community.

2 The Blended Librarian in Action

Applying Design Thinking to Academic Librarianship

> *Design is one of the basic characteristics of what it is to be human, and an essential determinant of the quality of human life. It affects everyone in every detail of every aspect of what they do throughout the day. As such, it matters profoundly.* —John Heskett

OBJECTIVES

1. Recognize the basic concepts of design and develop a design philosophy that can guide and inform the practices of academic librarians.
2. Gain familiarity with academic librarianship by design and with the importance of design thinking.
3. Understand the idea of designing a library experience to add value and further integrate the academic library into the teaching and learning process.

WHERE BLENDED LIBRARIANSHIP AND DESIGN THINKING INTERSECT

Having gained some exposure to blended librarianship and those who practice it, we want to further explore some basic aspects of design and how blended librarianship intersects with design thinking. As you can see from the profiles of blended librarians in the previous chapter, each in their own way has discovered the value of integrating some design practice into their work as librarians. In this chapter we will explore some principles of design and delve further into the concept of design thinking. Design thinking can sometimes be difficult to grasp. At its core there are three basic elements:

The ability to put oneself in the place of the user of the product or service in order to understand how the user can receive the optimal learning experience

A willingness to thoughtfully and creatively move through a series of gradual changes in developing a product or service and use this prototyping method to arrive at an optimal experience for the user

A commitment to both formative and summative evaluation in determining how well a product or service meets the needs of the user, and then making the necessary adjustments to improve the performance of that product or service to ensure a good library or learning experience for the user

Blended librarians are able to weave each of these three elements into their practice primarily by integrating instructional design and technology skills into their work. As they do, they are using design thinking to develop an instructional product or a new service innovation to benefit their end-user community. It is in the creation of products or services that the intersection between blended librarianship and design thinking occurs. Applying a design thinking mentality to a project to develop a self-guided learning tutorial, for example, would require a blended librarian to first get to know more about those students using the tutorial. The first task is to learn and understand what the students need to fill their information gap. Once equipped with this knowledge about the users and their needs, the product developer can design a prototype solution that can be tested and revised until it sufficiently accomplishes the task of helping the students fill their information gap. And finally, the blended librarian can study how users used the tutorial and can learn in what ways it failed to perform to expectations. From this the blended librarian's evaluation of the tutorial leads to an improved learning experience for the end users.

These are the ways that academic librarians incorporate design thinking into their work and in so doing contribute to their growth as blended librarians. Before we delve deeper into our understanding of design and design thinking, we will first examine the physical aspects of design with which many of us are quite familiar. What makes design so captivating is that the principles can be applied nicely to a range of practices and performances. Ultimately, our goal is to apply them to academic librarianship.

THE PHYSICAL WORLD OF DESIGN

It is true that design matters. Each individual's world is affected on a daily basis by the design that shapes our physical environment. Design is many different things. It can depend on an individual's profession, the personal paradigm he or she brings to an understanding of design, and the conceptual lenses with which the individual analyzes design. It can also depend on the context in which design is being discussed. A discussion about design between interior designers and instructional designers would seem worlds apart. When most of us think about design, we usually do so in terms of our physical environment. It may focus on our clothing, cars, or our office furniture.

In library settings, design may bring to mind a fairly common element of our existence: the structure and layout of our physical space. How well are our facilities laid out? Where should the circulation desk be, and is the reference desk too large and cumbersome? Do a search on the term *design* in the library literature, and you'll find a set of articles about the architecture and planning of library buildings or their interiors. Top professional publications such as *Library Journal* and *American Libraries* typically have annual issues related to design that focus on new and renovated library buildings.

The intention of this book is to explore facets of design beyond those limited to the interiors and exteriors of facilities. Still, this should in no way deny or minimize the critical importance of designing settings that contribute to and maximize a successful library experience for those using the physical facility. Vast amounts of attention have been paid to the importance of creating an environment that draws in the user community. Several years ago the *Chronicle of Higher Education* featured an article about the "deserted academic library." It suggested college and university students were no longer using their academic library. That article sparked numerous debates about the physical library building in a digital world. More important, it brought renewed awareness of an academic library that is more than an organized set of electronic resources.

A successful library needs to be a social, cultural, and intellectual center of the campus that makes positive contributions to its community. Enough cannot be said about the ways in which a well-designed building, outside and in, facilitates community building. Creating an inviting facility that lends itself to the demands and needs of a user community results in innovations such as information commons, well-designed and laid-out collaborative learning spaces, coffee shops, designated display and gallery space, and all the other hallmarks of well-designed contemporary library buildings. Information architecture is the view of the library from its users' vantage point. The best information architecture is one that is completely intuitive and predictable to the user. It makes perfect sense: design our spaces and signs so that our users can find things and find help easily (Dempsey 2005). One of this chapter's case studies focuses on how a design firm, MAYA Design, applied design thinking to the reinvention of the Carnegie Library's space; consult their PowerPoint slide presentation at http://www.carnegielibrary.org/presentations/jackson/userexppart2_files/frame.htm.

ACADEMIC LIBRARIANSHIP BY DESIGN

Though the interior and exterior perspectives on design must be recognized, an entirely different universe about design thinking exists that can contribute to the success of the academic library's user community. At its core, design can be strongly connected to basic values of academic librarianship: those that help create an environment that contributes to the success of faculty and students. These values are the passion that academic librarians bring to exploring ways in which they can exceed their past performance, both as individuals and as members of a library organization. This chapter will introduce some of the basic concepts of design that apply to the work of academic librarians.

Initially, this chapter will discuss design in general terms in an effort to provide a better grasp of what is meant by design, and in what ways it affects many different products and services. The chapter draws upon both theory and practice to illustrate the ways in which design is perceived and applied. We will introduce the idea of academic librarianship by design as a working philosophy that identifies those ways in which design can inform our practice and lead us to approach our work with thoughtfulness and structure. This takes the concept of design beyond the physical and into the intellectual realm of integrating the library into the teaching and learning process. Design thinking is a process by which academic librarians examine their services and resources to identify ways in which these can be improved and enhanced to reduce barriers to access for students and faculty.

Design is defined in many ways. By one definition it is the conscious examination of objects and processes to determine how they can be made better. Librarians may not create objects in the same way a floral designer produces a bouquet or an industrial designer fashions a lamp, but we can create objects for learning through a design process. Librarians also create services, and design firms are now assisting service organizations to reengineer their services for improved user experiences. Consider the progression of the library tutorial, with the advancement of instructional technologies, from static paper handouts to interactive, multimedia, web-based learning tools. The constant reshaping and redesigning of our libraries, their services, and their resources in the search for a better educational environment is in some ways the essence of the practice of academic librarianship. Poor design results in interfaces and instructional products that are hard to use, or services that fail to achieve what they were intended to do. This is the sense and meaning of *design* that we draw on for the design philosophy underlying what we refer to as "academic librarianship by design," or ALD.

In academic librarianship by design, the practitioner adopts design thinking. Just as *design* itself can take on multiple meanings, so too can *design thinking*. How it is described or what it involves may depend on whether the description is influenced by a business, design, engineering, anthropological, or other disciplinary perspective. Design thinking truly comes out of a multidisciplinary or hybrid school of thought. A design thinker will blend skills from a mix of disciplines. For example, a design thinker's initial idea for an innovation may emerge from the world of computing technology. The design thinker may apply some ethnographic research techniques to learn more about the users of the new technology product or service. Then business methods could be applied to promote or market a new information product. Finally, the design thinker may draw on education for evaluation methods. Those new to design thinking may experience it through multiple lenses of perception.

What are some common ways in which design thinking is described? What does it mean for the average person? What are the commonalities among the different interpretations of design thinking? Some design thinkers focus on the study and understanding of people and the ways in which they use products and services. To better design a product, for example, the designers put themselves in the place of the people who use that product. They use an empathetic or thoughtful approach in which they seek to understand the needs of the user. Other design thinkers focus more on innovative design and the application of design to the development of new and quite different products. Another commonly described aspect of design thinking is prototyping: taking a new service or product through multiple iterations of design and testing until it effectively meets the needs of the user. Design thinkers try to quickly get their idea into a prototype so that it can be further shaped through testing and feedback cycles (Brown 2005).

As blended librarians we bring our own special and unique perspective to design thinking. At the core of our interpretation, both people and innovation are the critical focus points. We believe that instructional design is particularly appropriate for developing a design thinking mentality in education-related professions. Instructional design retains some core elements of other design thinking interpretations—understanding the user, a thoughtful approach, prototyping, and new product innovation—but it focuses on a model referred to as ADDIE. We will explore the ADDIE model in more detail in chapter 3. To this we add the theory and practice of library science, our native discipline. We describe design thinking as a means of inquiry by which practitioners realize and give shape to their ideas about services and instructional products. It is mostly a process of thoughtful questioning and conceptually determining how library organizations can create better library experiences for their user communities. Design thinking is characterized by examining whether a library service is needed by its user community before physically designing and implementing the service; design thinkers put user needs ahead of their own technological interests. And if it seems that users could benefit from a new service, design thinking encourages the shaping of that process or service through prototyping and user feedback. And as instructional designers do, we place significant emphasis on both formative and summative evaluation in our interpretation of design thinking.

Academic librarianship by design is a departure from the traditional view of design in librarianship. Rather than focusing on the interiors and exteriors of library buildings, it is a process by which we examine our thinking about the services we provide, particularly as it relates to teaching and learning, connecting with our user community, and transforming ourselves and our resources. In the first decade of this new century, the academic library profession finds itself to some extent threatened with marginalization. No one is suggesting the impending demise of academic librarianship, but new information competitors are causing dramatic shifts in the patterns of users' information-seeking behavior. Where they may once have consulted the academic library as their first source for a research assignment, students and faculty now begin their research with an Internet search engine. As for search itself, users have radically different expectations about how those systems should look and work; academic libraries are frequently challenged to satisfy those expectations. For quick reference, even librarians consult reference books with far less frequency than at any time in the past, instead going straight to search engines for faster results.

Academic librarianship by design is about more than confronting marginalization. It is about an approach to librarianship that is guided by creative thinking and contemplation about what we do and how we do it. It is about exploring new resources and new technologies and reflecting on how they fit into the library's culture and yield specified outcomes before adopting them. It is about designing both objects—particularly digital materials that enhance learning—and experiences. Those objects and experiences should advance the library user's ability to conduct high-quality research. They should also engage the user in something that is memorable and creates a persistent change in his or her knowledge. This type of experience rarely happens in a single occurrence. It is the outcome of a larger, more encompassing design that the academic library creates for its user community. There are many different ways in which academic librarianship by design can manifest itself. We will explore them in this book, but there are no doubt many variations on this theme. Ultimately, it is you the reader who will determine how and in what ways you apply a design philosophy at your own institution.

We have developed the following statements to establish the general principles of academic librarianship by design:

ALD is the thoughtful application of traditional library skills and a knowledge of instructional design and technology skills to the discovery and development of tools that facilitate and enhance the integration of the library into the teaching and learning process.

ALD is the outcome of design thinking by academic librarians. Academic librarians will benefit from the study and implementation of design in their work.

ALD focuses on the creation of a library experience that allows the user community to do more than just superficially interact with the library; academic library users should have a deeper learning experience of gathering, organizing, and analyzing information in the pursuit and acquisition of new knowledge.

ALD is characterized by thoughtful and continuous improvement by academic librarians to develop better resources and services.

ALD may be applied to the design of interior and exterior library environments, but it primarily applies to the design of experiences that create better connections between academic librarians and their user community.

WHAT CONSTITUTES DESIGN

Design is a unique term in our language. Consider the following sentence used here to convey its breadth and depth:

Design is to design a design to produce a design.

The sentence is grammatically correct. The first use is a noun and relates to the field as a whole, as in "Design is a popular field of study for millennial generation students." The second use is as a verb, indicating a process or action, as in "Our library staff is about to design a new tutorial." The third use is also a noun but differs from the first in that here it refers to a concept or proposal, as in "The design for the new information commons was approved by the provost." And the final use is a noun once again, indicating a complete product, as in "The latest tutorial is our best design yet" (Heskett 2002).

Another perspective on design suggests that it occurs in three different spheres. First, it can relate to the design of specific products, as in the use of *design* as a noun described in the previous paragraph. Industrial designers create specific products such as furniture, car interiors, or tape dispensers. The second sphere is environmental design, or the design of place. This is perhaps the most common perception of design and is the one most familiar to the academic library profession. Building and landscape architects, as well as interior designers, create internal and external environments. The final grouping of design is communication, or the design of messages. This third category is perhaps the broadest and vaguest of all. Yet it perhaps best encompasses the type of design that most accurately fits what academic librarians do. We design environments to help our user communities connect with information, and we thus facilitate communication between end users and their intended audiences. Communication depends on media. Media serve to transmit messages from one source to another. Academic librarians can acquire or create media or design larger-scale media that help library users use the library environment more effectively (Potter 2002).

A word with so many different meanings and interpretations can confuse. Adding to the nebulous aura of design is the breadth of ways in which it is practiced. Consider just a few of the practices that fall under the design umbrella: industrial design, interior design, graphic design, digital design, fashion design, and software design. A portal to design information called Design Directory (http://www.dexigner.com/directory/) lists over 4,000 links to design-related sites and categorizes them into more than forty-five types of design. Many of the design fields found on this site are more about ways to communicate professional competence than they are academic disciplines. Examples can include floral design, food design, advertising design, and craft design.

Why no library design? Our profession has its roots in the design of systems that facilitate the organization and retrieval of information, but it has preferred to adopt the term *library science* to describe its theoretical foundations as well as its practice. Referring back to the multiple meanings of the term *design,* library design traditionally implies the concept or proposal for a new or renovated facility. Academic librarianship by design takes on an alternate meaning for design. It seeks to emphasize the verb or action meaning of the term. When we speak about academic librarianship by design, we mean to describe a process for the design of library experiences or the information products that contribute to that experience. The broadest definition of *design* can certainly encompass much of what the library profession does: design is the shaping and making of the environment by humans to give it meaning and serve our needs (Heskett 2002). Our libraries and their services and resources are constructs designed to help others create meaning in their lives and to provide a learning experience.

NEW WAYS OF THINKING ABOUT DESIGN

In the world of management guru Tom Peters, design is so critical that it should be on the agenda of every meeting in every single department. Peters is a design fanatic who has been known to say, "Everything is design" (Reingold 2003). There is ample evidence that design as a concept and guiding philosophy is expanding into new fields and disciplines beyond its traditional artistic roots. Business is making design the byword of leadership and management. Because of the growing recognition of its power to affect human behavior, increasing numbers of organization specialists think executives should adopt a design perspective (Farson 2005). Good advice, but how might members of the library profession adopt a design perspective? To our way of thinking, one way is to begin learning about design, and reading this book is a good start.

Since our own field is perhaps just at the cusp of discovering design outside of the traditional building perspective, one way to develop a design perspective is to see how other fields and professions are exploring ways in which design can influence thought and action. Business in particular is catching on to the importance of design, and one source of influence is the field of industrial and product design. Consider the fact that Stanford University established an Institute of Design to teach design thinking and strategy to business and engineering students. Traditionally business has largely been about the management and administration of organizations. But contemporary business places a premium on creativity and innovation. That is a primary reason why the world of business seeks to understand and apply design thinking, because design is a creative art that is largely about developing innovations and improvements. As Sara Beckman, a professor at the Haas School of Business of the University of California at Berkeley, said, "Traditional business is about focusing on solving a problem, but the design process focuses on problem finding" (Merritt and Lavelle 2005).

More concrete examples of design are found frequently in *Business Week*'s "Innovate and Design" supplement. It features excellent profiles of firms and individuals that are using design thinking to transform their businesses, introduce new products, or simply generate more innovation. A previous issue of this supplement (found online at http://www.businessweek.com/innovate/index.html), for example, explored how Kodak is moving, after having reinvented itself for the digital camera market, into the digital photo-processing market where it hopes to be the Apple of digital photography. This is more than an example of product design. It's an example of model design, which is to say that Kodak and other firms must reinvent their core business model. Apple is often the poster child for model reinvention because it moved strictly from product, to distribution, and ultimately to providing an incomparable user experience. Librarians would do well to learn from these experiences and apply them to redesigning their own business model.

A business-oriented definition of *design* was developed by the marketing guru Philip Kotler, another believer in the importance of design for strategic business advantage. He said that design is "the process of seeking to optimize consumer satisfaction and company profitability through the creative use of major design elements (performance, quality, durability, appearance, and cost) in connection with products, environments, information, and corporate identities" (Kotler and Rath 1984). With a bit of tweaking, that definition can apply to academic libraries. We certainly want to optimize the user's satisfaction, and our motive is deeper learning rather than profit. We too can creatively develop those design elements to benefit our user communities. As library-experience designers, Kotler would say we must have a clear sense of what services and resources our users want from us, and we must then create them in ways that perform to users' expectations. Whatever we create must be of high quality and be sustainable (durable) in nature. Appearance can certainly apply to the interior and exterior of libraries, but it can also apply to the interfaces of our resources; they will not be used if their appearance is less than sensible. And just like other designers, we must work within our budgets.

One of the most influential books about design thinking is *The Art of Innovation.* Coauthor Tom Kelley is the general manager of Silicon Valley–based IDEO, one of the world's leading product design firms. IDEO is perhaps best known for designing the Apple mouse and the Palm handheld, along with hundreds of other cutting-edge products and services. The reason business so readily grasped Kelley's book is its messages about fostering cultures and processes for continuous improvement and innovation. The Apple mouse is a good example. IDEO didn't invent it; they simply created a next-generation version. From examining how people used the mouse, to rethinking the contours of the bumps in its surface and even the injection molding process used to shape the mouse, IDEO just improved on an existing design and development process. But the question everyone had was, "How do they do it?" The answer: design thinking.

While it may not apply in every library situation, Kelley does identify the five key elements of what he calls "the IDEO method."

Understand—Get to know the needs and challenges of your user population and how they perceive your products and services.

Observe—Watch real people in real-life situations to find out how they work, what confuses them, what they like and dislike, and where their needs can be better served. (See the MAYA Design case study at the end of this chapter.)

Visualize—Think about new ideas and concepts and how the people who use your library will use them. Kelley dedicates an entire chapter to IDEO's brainstorming process for visualizing new designs.

Evaluate and Refine—IDEO invests heavily in the prototyping process in order to test ideas and then improve them. Prototyping is also an important part of the instructional design process, as is formative evaluation.

Implement—This is often the longest and most difficult part of the process, but it is how any new product or service goes public for user consumption.

IDEO has used this process to develop everything from toys to highly advanced medical products that save people's lives. The challenge for a profession such as academic librarianship is to figure out how we can adapt the IDEO method of design thinking to create another emerging concept: the library experience. While academic librarians will likely never design an industrial product such as a computer mouse, there are two things we can and should be designing: library instructional products and better library experiences for our user communities.

In this second chapter we have identified the many levels on which design takes place. To summarize, they can occur in three general ways: product, environment, and communication. While all of these types of design could in some way contribute to the design of a library experience, academic librarianship by design focuses on taking a thoughtful and creative approach to designing library resources, services, and learning experiences. These three, combined, all contribute to the overall library experience.

THE LIBRARY EXPERIENCE

Design is about more than designing products and environments. Airports do not have a specific product, but they do provide an experience: the one that you have when you need to travel by air. Most of us would likely describe that experience as unpleasant, stressful, and in other negative ways. In *The Art of Innovation* Kelley describes the idea of designing an "experience." Kelley states that any service can be designed as a better experience. Think about a bad experience when you go somewhere, and ask how that experience might be improved. Academic libraries will never be Las Vegas when it comes to providing an entertaining or exciting experience, but if the Pike Place Fish Market in Seattle can make buying fish an experience, can't academic librarians create a better library experience?

The good news is that academic librarians realized several years ago that if they didn't provide a better user experience, then students and faculty would go elsewhere. With respect to our physical and virtual environments, progress is being made. Those libraries having the ability to do so have added more space for serious study and socialization. Any library that could has added a café or other means for users to obtain food and beverages and has reduced or eliminated strict rules about bringing refreshments into the library. There is a renewed emphasis on improved signage and better customer service so that library users can find what they need when they need it and get responsive, respectful assistance. The MAYA Design project at the Carnegie Library of Pittsburgh was all about creating a better user experience, and that project should be studied by librarians wanting to improve the library's physical environment. Dozens of articles and presentations have addressed the importance of conducting a usability study to evaluate the library's website for ease of use and clarity. The signs point to a growing emphasis on transforming the academic library into a cultural, social, and intellectual environment, physically and virtually, that provides the campus community with an efficient and educational experience, much like the type of experience advocated by Tom Kelley of IDEO.

Academic librarianship by design seeks to create the library experience in two areas that will present greater challenges than enhancing the library building or website. The first is integrating the library into the teaching and learning process, and the second is adding value to the process of using the academic library for research and discovery. Achieving these types of library experiences will be more difficult for a variety of reasons that relate to the academic librarian's relationship with his or her user community. Enhanced integration into the teaching and learning process requires the collaboration of faculty; partnerships with faculty are the keystone to connecting with students in their physical and virtual learning spaces.

But faculty are busy and often overwhelmed with their own teaching, service, and research responsibilities. Working together with librarians to create more effective research assignments or to discover ways to encourage their students to use the library's resources is far from the highest priority for many faculty. Students are less convinced than ever that they need what their academic library offers. With user expectations being shaped by Internet information resources that offer an entirely different user experience, one that instantly gratifies and requires little in the way of critical thought from those searching for information, designing a library experience that will balance the need for simplicity while resolving complex information needs presents real challenges.

Before you write off the idea of a library experience as just another faddish marketing concept, you should know that we agree that calling something an experience doesn't make it an experience. We subscribe to the understanding of creating a genuinely good experience as advocated by Mark Hurst, creator of GoodExperience.com. Creating a library experience or any other "experience," according to Hurst, comes down to working to create something good, something of value that is bigger than your own involvement and context. This really is what academic librarianship by design is about: using design thinking to continuously improve our resources and services with the goal of creating a learning experience for the library user. It is much more than referring to your library as an "experience" while actually doing little to create something good for the user.

A MINDMAP OF THE BLENDED LIBRARIAN'S PERSPECTIVE

This chapter is primarily about the basics of design and the concept of design thinking. These principles are central to the practice of academic librarianship by design, but we realize the material might seem largely theoretical or external to librarianship. How would an academic librarian go about putting some of these ideas into practice, and how would he or she operationalize this idea of design thinking? We began this chapter by establishing the connection between blended librarians and design thinking. Blended librarianship provides a useful framework for the practice of academic librarianship by design. The blended librarian's perspective on academic librarianship by design identifies ways in which these ideas can become a part of our practice.

A grasp of design philosophy will be useful to any librarian who would like to adopt some of the principles and practices of blended librarianship. Throughout this book we will present examples of the ways in which a blended librarian brings his or her design skills to address one of the significant goals in making the academic library more essential to its user community: integrating the library into the teaching and learning process. We acknowledge that academic librarianship encompasses a wide range of different skills and workplace functionalities. Can blended librarianship make a difference in all the different areas in which librarians are working, be it cataloging, acquisitions, collection management, or reference? We believe that academic librarianship by design, because it focuses on applying design thinking to the thoughtful and creative improvement of library processes and practices, can be applied by any academic librarian no matter what functions he or she performs. As the famed designer Milton Glaser said, "Anything purposeful can be called an act of design."

However, our intention with blended librarianship is to provide librarians with tools and techniques to better integrate the library into the teaching and learning process. Hence, the applications we will discuss in this book will be most applicable to those librarians who help students and faculty to learn how to use the library to improve the quality of research. Consider the mindmap shown in figure 2-1, which we designed to illustrate our conceptualization of academic librarianship by design from the blended librarian's perspective.

A mindmap is an instructional technologist's visual representation of one's interpretation and understanding of a process, why it exists, and its ultimate outcome. For the individual, the mindmap helps to define the process and give sense to it. A mindmap for librarianship, for example, could have at its core such ideals as free access to information for personal achievement or providing the foundation for a free society. In the mindmap shown in figure 2-1, creating a better library

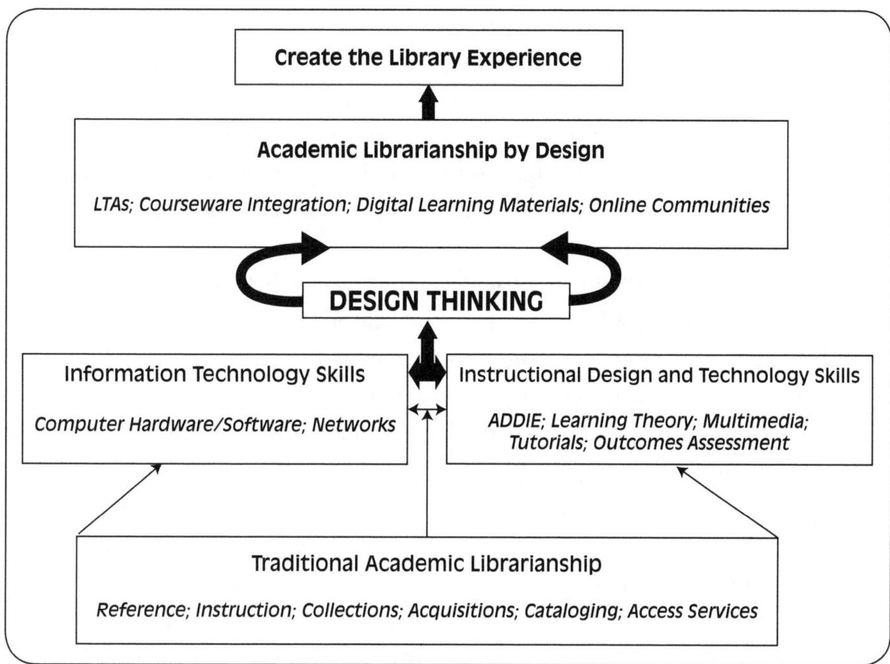

FIGURE 2-1
Mindmap for academic librarianship by design

experience for the end user is the ultimate outcome of academic librarianship by design. The three main skill sets that combine to form blended librarianship are at the base of the mindmap. With the application of design thinking to the mix, the blended librarian develops the library experience in his or her own institution.

CASE STUDIES

The following are the first of several groups of case studies provided throughout this book in order to supply the reader with more concrete examples of how design thinking is being put into practice within the library profession.

The Redesign of the Carnegie Library of Pittsburgh

CONTRIBUTED BY ARADHANA GOEL

The Carnegie Library of Pittsburgh, the oldest public library system in the country, wanted to regain its place as a relevant, accessible, and usable information system on a par with the current favorites: Amazon.com and Google in the digital world and Barnes and Noble in the physical world. The goal was to transform the library from a dark, dusty, and confusing environment to a bright, inviting place that would be attentive to customers and teeming with up-to-date information. This transformation project was conceived as an interdisciplinary and collaborative endeavor with MAYA Design as information technology architects, along with building renovation architects, librarians, the library's IT department, and other consultants.

MAYA's biggest challenge (and achievement) was to help a traditional institution make deep organizational changes and adopt technological advances. The key takeaway for the library was the information architecture, which was scalable for systemwide organizational change and extensible for ongoing evolution.

MAYA's architects began their work by trying to understand library users' mental model and the library's organizational schemes. They evaluated the library environment against usability guidelines, using well-established processes like focus groups, shadowing, direct observation, personas, and so on, and customized processes like guerrilla ethnography and breakpoint analysis. Their research showed that the Carnegie Library had institutionalized a disjointed system (a feature-centric approach). The digital, the physical, and the human aspects of the library experience had evolved separately with a focus on ease of maintenance rather than ease of use.

As part of their ethnographic/contextual research, they "walked a mile in the customers' shoes" and documented their experiences using creative storyboarding techniques. MAYA defined the information architecture—a blueprint of the library's components and patterns of user interaction with those components. They identified three classes of information organizers: space, people, and categorizations (such as the Library of Congress, the Dewey decimal system, etc.). When users interacted with these organizers, they encountered problems and breakpoints. Critical breakpoints occurred not only within each organizer interface but also when users traversed between them.

The breakpoints revealed inconsistencies that repeatedly stumped users. Library jargon had permeated the space, and decades of ad hoc solutions had resulted in layers of counterintuitive solutions. The "environmental complexity" (information overload of sights, sounds, and signs) confused and intimidated users. There was a lack of intuitive continuity from one organizer to another. For example, users had difficulty mapping the location of a book in a catalog to its location on the physical shelf.

Based on the inherent strengths and weaknesses of each of these organizers, MAYA developed "principles of design" that would build necessary bridges and help users move seamlessly from one interface to another—making their experience rewarding. These principles became the common design and communication platform for library stakeholders and all participating consultants in the project.

MAYA also developed a dynamic information system for the library—a family of electronic signs that would provide a uniform yet flexible way to "publish" timely, appropriate information. Their work included

- defining a consistent lexicon for all the libraries
- designing a classification scheme for way finding, educational, and marketing information
- collaborating with architects and signage consultants to implement this scheme in different library branches
- creating a publish-on-demand content management system for both electronic and paper-based signs

Architects, planners, librarians, and sign fabricators used this system to produce a consistent signage system that was appropriate to the location and function of library service areas. Even though the designs, ages, and renovation plans of the various library branches vary greatly, the multiple branches in the system now work as one cohesive experience (from the customers' perspective).

As a result, the Carnegie Library has begun reclaiming its place as a valued, innovative, and inspiring center of information and discovery. The physical changes brought about by architectural renovations have been matched and enhanced by a complementary overhaul of how the library serves its customers. Changed perceptions have attracted new customers who would have otherwise avoided the library. Existing customers find it easier to accomplish their goals and, along the way, discover new things that they might otherwise have missed. Librarians and library staff devote more of their time to high-value, high-reward efforts. Administrators can now make long-term plans based on a flexible and well-structured framework.

For images related to this project, see the PowerPoint slide presentation at http://www.carnegielibrary.org/presentations/jackson/userexppart2_files/frame.htm.

This section was contributed by MAYA Design, information design and technology consultants (core team: Mickey McManus, Aradhana Goel, Paul Gould, Mike Higgins, Heather McQuaid). Included with permission by Sheila Jackson, assistant director, Main Library Services, Carnegie Library of Pittsburgh. Project architects/signage consultants: EDGE Studios, architects for the Main Library in Oakland, Pittsburgh; Arthur Lubetz, architects for the Squirrel Hill Branch Library, Pittsburgh; Landesberg Design, signage consultants for branch libraries.

The Undergraduate Research Project at the University of Rochester

CONTRIBUTED BY VICKI BURNS, UNIVERSITY OF ROCHESTER

What do undergraduates really do when they write research papers? In searching for answers, librarians at the University of Rochester's River Campus Libraries developed the Undergraduate Research Project to gain a clearer understanding of how today's "Internet generation" students live and work on our campus.

The University of Rochester (New York), established in 1850, is a private research university with 7,000 students and approximately 1,000 faculty. About 4,000 undergraduates live on the largely residential campus. The Undergraduate Research Project is an outgrowth of the River Campus Libraries' user-based approach to designing services. A work practice study of the faculty was conducted in 2003 by lead anthropologist Nancy Fried Foster as part of the campus planning for an institutional repository. One outcome of this project was the development of competence across library departments in work practice techniques, and a commitment to using a "codesign" process with our users, whether the project is for undergraduates, graduate students, faculty, or library staff.

In fall 2004 the Undergraduate Research Project was launched by a cross-departmental team under the guidance of Foster. As a prestudy, subject librarians interviewed faculty to learn more about research/writing assignments and their expectations for student work. Understanding faculty expectations and appreciating the variation across disciplines provided a foundation for our research. We then interviewed students who had just completed a research paper. Students told us how they wrote their papers and drew simple pictures of each step along the way. We paid particular attention to how students sequenced activities, selected resources, sought help, and completed assignments. We were interested in where students worked, the times of day they were active, the people they talked with, the problems they encountered, and the help they received. We were also interested in the more general information we collected about student life, especially regarding the use of such tools as computers, PDAs, cell phones, and other communication devices; text-editing and other software; and recreational technology (MP3 players, gaming systems, etc.). When we first observed Foster interviewing students, we realized that our past surveys had focused on our desire to evaluate library programs. Now our focus shifted and we were learning about students' lives and the way they approach their studies.

The interviews were the first of several techniques used in our research. We held design workshops to gather student opinions about the libraries' website and space planning. The students caught the spirit of the project and provided fresh perspectives for us. Their "ideal" web page has our web team busy rethinking the purpose and design of the libraries' web presence. In another workshop, twenty-six students sketched layouts for a large public space in the main library scheduled for renovation. It seemed as if they had been waiting for the opportunity to tell us what they wanted.

Another idea garnered from watching the interviews was to conduct observations of specific physical spaces and facilities at varying times and places in the libraries. Building signage and the extent of laptop use were two areas that particularly interested us. Research team members also visited dorms late at night to videotape and interview students in their living and working spaces. The students were happy to show our team what they were doing with their computers and how they organized their work space.

Other research methods gave us insight into the daily routines of students' lives. Some students kept map diaries in which they tracked a day's comings and goings on a campus map. Others marked the places on campus that they liked and disliked, felt comfortable or uncomfortable in. Students created photographic journals by taking pictures of their rooms, where they studied, their friends, objects they carried all the time, and other specified places and objects. Some students wrote intellectual self-reports providing a picture of who they are intellectually and how they got that way.

Our formal research ended in late summer 2006. Well before then, the library staff reported they had a better understanding of how students live and work. Here are a few comments from our final team meeting:

> [I] like the rapport we had with the students—conversations were lively and comfortable.
>
> [The] student experience is both much like it was thirty years ago and vastly different—especially in patterns of communication and multitasking.
>
> [I] appreciated getting actual data on how students work rather than guesses and hearsay.
>
> One of the best things was videotaping in the dorms.
>
> [I] loved that so many staff were involved—this changed our organizational culture.

Putting ideas garnered from the research into practice is happening naturally. The student sketches from design workshops are integral in planning a renovation scheduled for fall 2007 completion. For example, the designers and architects planned to place upholstered seating around large windows, but the students definitely prefer study tables in that natural light. The latest sketches show tables near the windows.

Students were critical of the libraries' website. They envisioned an individualized web space with connections to all the university sites integral to their busy lives, for example, registrar, bursar, library, classes, clubs. Such a student portal is currently being developed in partnership with University Technology Services.

Our research shows that a typical student schedule is tilted toward late evening to early morning. As a result, "night owl" librarians work at the reference desk later than usual during the busiest weeks of the semester. We are willing to accommodate the students' schedules to 11 p.m. So far no one has volunteered to work at the reference desk until the library closes at 3 a.m.

Since we learned that students consult with parents about their papers, we decided that making the parents aware of our programs would be another way to reach students. The library hosted the parents' breakfast during student orientation, where we promoted our subject librarians with the theme of "a librarian for every class." The breakfast was a great success. And the director of orientation was pleased (and relieved) to hand the responsibility for this early morning event over to us.

One sobering discovery was that of students' lack of understanding about the role of reference librarians. We are trying new approaches to this old challenge. We now have librarian-tutors working in the College Writing Center and are developing technology to improve the connections to research tools in subject guides and course pages. This issue is not as easily solved as moving sofas away from windows, but it is one that remains foremost in our planning.

This is just the beginning. The results of this research will continue to influence our decisions. We are also confident that we have firmly embraced the techniques necessary to ensure that future decisions are informed by the ways our students live and work.

CONCLUSION

We believe that librarians in all types of academic settings already practice some elements of design thinking, even if they have yet to become aware that they do so. Ours is a profession that constantly produces new ideas and innovations. If academic librarians were to think more purposefully about design, it could lead to a more directed effort toward continuous improvement and innovation. In the coming chapters, we will discuss topics (e.g., CMS/LMS, DLMs, LTAs) that relate back to the theme of this book, and we will explore how these techniques and technologies can help to integrate the library into the teaching and learning process, as well as add value to the process of using the library for research and discovery. We believe that as this book deconstructs the process of design in academic librarianship, more academic librarians will become conscious of the benefits that design can provide to the development and delivery of our services and resources. This was once the case with certain business processes, such as quality control, before thinkers such as W. Edward Deming figured out what it was and how to improve it. As Tim Brown of IDEO has said, "The same thing needs to happen with design. Organizations need to take design thinking seriously . . . not because design is magic or wondrous, but simply because by focusing on it, we'll make it better" (Brown 2005). We believe the same thing needs to happen with academic librarianship by design. By exploring it, providing a framework by which we can apply it in practice, identifying appropriate methods, and highlighting some of the pioneering work that is influenced by design thinking, we hope our readers will be encouraged to adopt it as an integral part of their professional practice.

TOPICS FOR FURTHER DISCUSSION

Prior to reading this chapter, what did the word *design* mean to you? How has this chapter changed your thinking about design?

Can you describe an example from an academic library in which you worked that would illustrate a resource or service that was introduced without much thought to its design? How well was that resource or service received? How might have more thought to its design have helped the service?

What aspects of design thinking do you think would be most critical to blended librarianship?

ADDITIONAL RESOURCES

Design Management Institute. http://www.dmi.org.

Experience Design Resources. http://www.nathan.com/ed/index.html.

Hempel, Jessi, and Aili McConnon. 2006. "The Talent Hunt." *Business Week* 4004 (October 9): 66–72.

IDEO company website. http://www.ideo.com.

IDesign: Seven Ways of Design Thinking. http://www.idesignthinking.com.

Martin, Roger. 2006. "Tough Love: Business Wants to Love Design but It's Often an Awkward Romance." *Fast Company* 109 (October): 54–58.

Pethokoukis, James M. 2006. "The Deans of Design: From the Computer Mouse to the Newest Swiffer, IDEO Is the Firm behind the Scenes." *U.S. News and World Report* 141 (October 2): 65–68.

3 ADDIE
Putting the Design in Academic Librarianship by Design

Design moves things from an existing condition to a preferred one.

—Milton Glaser

OBJECTIVES

1. Introduce the theory and practice of instructional design.
2. Familiarize the reader with the phases of an instructional design process known as ADDIE.
3. Introduce a modified version of ADDIE for blended librarians.
4. Identify ways in which instructional design connects with design thinking for the enhancement of academic library practices.

FOCUS ON INSTRUCTIONAL DESIGN

To enhance their ability to support the instructional needs of faculty, some of the academic librarians profiled in the previous chapter obtained advanced degrees in instructional design and technology. Currently that's rare among librarians, but as their teaching role expands it is likely that more academic librarians will become "blended." When they do they will no doubt be integrating instructional design and technology skills into their jobs. Learning more about instructional design and technology also better equips academic librarians to communicate effectively with their institution's instructional designers and technologists. We can learn about instructional design from our institutional colleagues or enter into formal degree programs; either option moves an academic librarian in the direction of becoming more blended. As they engage in this process, one of the things that academic librarians will discover about instructional designers is that their approach to learning is unique, and that some of their theory and practice can influence how we design, develop, and implement better library services and resources for the user community.

In this chapter we will examine instructional design more closely. While blended librarianship is a mix of new skills, one of the most important ones is instructional design. Therefore, it is important that we devote this chapter to this topic to ensure that it is well understood and that it provides the reader with the necessary skills to engage in a design process at whatever level is desired. We also want to connect our discussion of design thinking to our understanding of instructional design. Design is the common theme, and the two share a similar goal: using creative and thoughtful processes to make improvements to a product or service. While it will ultimately result in moving from an existing condition to a preferred one, instructional design is a process that often begins with a problem that could most often be characterized as "Why isn't learning taking place?" or "What skills is our population lacking and how can we most effectively help them to learn those skills?"

IDENTIFYING LEARNING GAPS

How might this learning problem manifest itself in an academic library setting? Think about these possibilities:

Students in a specific disciplinary area or course who consistently produce poor papers owing to shoddy research or the routine use of low-quality source material

College seniors who are still unfamiliar with the scholarly journal literature in their discipline

Distance learning students who need better research skills but are unable to take advantage of the librarians' on-site user education programs that are restricted to the main campus

Faculty who indicate a willingness to more fully integrate information literacy skill building into their courses but who clearly lack the ability to adequately transfer the appropriate skills to their students

Library staff or student workers who need to learn a new technology in order to deliver better customer service as library service points

In all of these situations we could identify a learning gap. A learning gap is defined as the difference between the existing knowledge of the learners and the subject matters or skills that they need. The instructional designer's first task is to assess and analyze the learning problem to better understand it in order to develop a solution. While it's true that almost any course or workshop that is delivered could be said to fill a learning gap, and that many institutions employ instructional designers to aid faculty in the development of curricula and courses, academic librarians would more likely use instructional design to develop unique solutions to the type of learning situations described in the list above.

Academic librarians are certainly no strangers to developing instruction sessions and related support material, as well as online and computer-based tutorials. In this chapter we will refer to these learning materials as "instructional products." But often those products are created based on the librarians' own perception of what the learners need to know. They are not informed by an in-depth analysis or assessment of what the learners already know or what they really need to know. Moreover, academic librarians' instruction is rarely the result of a thoughtful design process but rather is quickly developed simply to provide a requested instruction session. This critique is not intended as an attack on academic librarians because they fail to use instructional design methods. Rather, it is intended to identify those ways in which their instruction can benefit from design thinking.

Recall that design thinking is a thoughtful questioning process that is used to give shape to services and instructional products. For example, before creating an information literacy tutorial, how often do librarians determine if their user community learns well through online instruction modules? How often do they use a prototyping process that seeks to obtain feedback from users in creating the tutorial? Is the process of developing a tutorial informed by what works best to solve the students' learning gap, or is the tutorial simply a technology solution to the librarian's own lack of time or ability to integrate instruction into the classroom learning process?

Many librarians are familiar with TILT, the Texas Information Literacy Tutorial. It was developed between 1996 and 1999 for the University of Texas library system. Many libraries since then have adopted TILT as their primary information literacy tutorial and modified it for local use. What many librarians may not realize is that TILT was created with the help of instructional designers who put many hours of labor into the development of the tutorial. As this chapter will reveal, true instructional design is a time-consuming process. We realize that academic librarians are unlikely to have the time needed for thorough instructional design and certainly would be incapable of integrating it at the level required of a project like TILT. But we do believe there are elements of the design process that, when informed by a design thinking perspective, can be used by most academic librarians to develop better-designed and better-functioning instructional products.

WHAT IS ADDIE?

At its root, instructional design is the process of solving instructional problems through a systematic analysis of the conditions for learning. It is derived from a combination of theories from the fields of psychology, systems design, and communication. The instructional designer's perspective is that learning should not occur in a haphazard manner (Seels and Glasgow 1998). Rather, it should happen as the result of an orderly process in which there are clearly stated outcomes that can be measured. Instructional design is also referred to as instructional systems design (ISD). A typical textbook on the subject would identify dozens of ISD models. What ties together nearly all forms of instructional systems design is a generic model known as ADDIE. It is an acronym for

Analysis—the process of defining what is to be learned

Design—the process of specifying how it is to be learned

Development—the process of authoring and producing learning materials

Implementation—the process of installing the instruction product in a real-world context

Evaluation—the process of determining the impact of the instruction

An instructional designer who works for a company that designs learning materials for corporations may spend hundreds of hours working as part of a larger design team to develop those materials. Few academic librarians have the necessary time to thoroughly and fully implement ADDIE in designing information literacy instruction. But we believe that when academic librarians adopt the instructional designer's mind-set, it is possible to develop an understanding of learning needs that is the first step on the path to the thoughtful, organized, and purposeful development and evaluation of instructional products that fill observed learning gaps.

Just to provide an illustration of how ADDIE permeates design of all types and in all places, consider this comparison between ADDIE and the "IDEO method" described in chapter 2 that is the process IDEO uses to develop its unique products.

ADDIE	**IDEO**
Analyze	Understand/Observe
Design/Develop	Visualize/Brainstorm
Implement	Implement
Evaluate	Evaluate/Refine

Even though the IDEO method is a more modern version of an instructional systems design process, on further inspection it can be shown to share its core elements with ADDIE. Within each element of ADDIE there are some additional pieces of design process that help to clarify what actually happens during ADDIE and also identify the types of information that are needed to move from the initial stages of analysis to the final evaluation. To provide a better understanding of the ADDIE model, each of the five steps in the process is discussed below in more detail in the context of information literacy learning challenges.

ANALYSIS: START BY ELIMINATING UNCERTAINTY

When presented with a new instructional challenge—for example, trying to help students in a junior-level science writing course develop better techniques for analyzing research questions and developing research strategies—the first step is to try to understand what the students already know and what they don't know. To best analyze the situation, a blended librarian needs to identify the learning gap. At this stage two questions are asked. The first is "What is the problem?" and the second is "How can it be fixed?" Obtaining the answers to these questions constitutes the first phase of the analysis process and is referred to as the needs analysis. The goal is to remove uncertainty about the learning gap before any attempt is made at developing the instructional product. Therefore, one of the first products developed in ADDIE is the problem statement.

Here's an example of a problem statement for the hypothetical science student research project:

> *Problem Statement:* Faculty who teach the junior-level science seminar increasingly find that the quality of their students' research papers is on the decline. A review of the students' papers suggests that there are two learning gaps at play here. First, the students seem to have a poor grasp of the process of developing research questions that can serve as the foundation of their papers. Second, there is a gap between the students' knowledge of the research tools and their ability to create a search strategy for their topic. Without an effective strategy it doesn't matter how rich the content is; students will likely fail at retrieving good articles for their research.

To summarize:

GAP ONE

a. What is: Junior-level science students are showing deficiencies in their ability to formulate research questions for their science research projects.
b. What should be: Junior-level science students will be able, without assistance from faculty or librarians, to articulate a research question that effectively serves as a guide for their work in databases and search engines.

GAP TWO

a. What is: Junior-level science students fail to formulate search strategies that can then accurately retrieve articles that are most relevant to their science project and its articulated search question.
b. What should be: Students will be able to create an effective search strategy prior to the searching of library and Internet databases.

The other two phases of the analysis process are task analysis and instructional analysis. Task analysis has its own special question, which is "What is the job?" In other words, what types of research tasks do the science students need to accomplish? The actual tasks involved would be examined in detail. In this stage, instructional designers often develop a flowchart that shows the steps students need to follow to accomplish the learning task. Task analysis can also seek to learn more about the task content. What materials will the students need to use in compiling or writing their research papers? The second stage is the instructional analysis. The focus of this step is to determine specifically what must be learned. Each task is scrutinized to identify what a person must learn to complete the task. The task analysis will also identify gaps between required competencies and what the learners already know.

Depending on the degree to which it is conducted, task analysis can be time-consuming and detail-laden. Here is an example of just two subparts of the task analysis for the students' research in a library database:

SUBTASK 2: Conduct Database Search

a. Choose the appropriate search interface.

SUB-SUBTASK 2A1: If search has a single concept term or two-word phrase, choose the basic search interface. If search has multiple concepts, terms, or phrases, use the advanced search interface.

Example of single concept: assessment
Example of phrase concept: information literacy
Example of multiple concept search: information literacy and assessment

b. Enter the search term(s) into the box(es) provided.

SUB-SUBTASK 2B1: When using the advanced search interface, enter each of the multiple concept terms into a single search box and retain the AND connector.

c. Choose additional search limiters if desired.

SUB-SUBTASK 2C1: If date limit is needed. enter date restriction. If full text only is desired, check off box. If peer review literature is desired, check off box.

d. Click the "search" button to initiate the search.

This level of analysis likely exceeds what most library practitioners have time for, but it does provide an idea of the type of work that task analysis involves. An optional part of the process, if desired, is to conduct a task survey in which an actual questionnaire would be distributed to the learners to find out what their needs are. The survey results can greatly inform the development of the task workflow. The goal is to truly understand what the learner is trying to accomplish before thinking one knows enough to develop an instructional product that offers a solution to the problem statement.

DESIGN: HOW THIS CONTENT CAN BEST BE TAUGHT

Next comes the design phase. In this stage the librarian would begin to think more deeply about how the learning gaps could best be filled. An instructional designer's approach would be to construct a design grid that will inform the development process. A design grid typically has three columns: objectives, assessment, and instructional strategy. Many library instructors proceed with their teaching before giving thought to these three dimensions of instruction, but they are critical to the development of a good instruction product or session. Think about it. If the learning objectives are unknown, how is it possible to assess if the learners acquired the desired skills? It is also important to think about the instructional method that best achieves the objective. The following are examples of the types of information needed for a design grid.

Objective. This describes a specific outcome that the learner will be able to accomplish as a result of engaging in the learning process. For example, here is a possible objective related to the science students' research paper: "After reading the faculty member's assignment, the students will be able to write a single English sentence that articulates a specific question that will be answered with a research process for all research assignments received during the course." There is no exact science to objective writing, but a frequently recommended technique is the A-B-C-D method in which four components of any objective are developed. A is for the audience; for whom is the instruction intended? B is for behavior; what behavior should the learner have at the end of the instruction? C is for condition; under what condition must the learner perform the skill? D is for degree; this establishes the standard for determining when the learner has achieved the objective. In the above objective, the audience is the junior-level science students. The behavior is the ability to convert an assignment into an articulated research question. The condition is somewhat vague in this objective, but it could be specified that the learner acquires the skill during the library instruction period while performing an exercise with a hands-on computing activity. D is typically stated as "learner achieves a score of 90 or greater" or "can accomplish the task nine of ten times." These components reflect a proficiency achievement, which may or may not make sense for an information literacy objective. The A-B-C-D method is a good framework for developing objectives, even though not every objective will always include one of each.

Assessment. This describes the method to be used for determining if the students have accomplished the objective during the learning process as a result of interacting with the instruction product. For example, the following describes a potential assessment method for the objective: "Given the assignment, students will spend fifteen minutes in class developing a research question that will be written on a sheet of paper and then submitted to the instructor. The librarian and instructor will review the research questions and return them to the students with comments for revisions, if needed."

Instructional Strategy. There are numerous media and instructional methods that can be mixed, matched, and selected to accomplish the objective. The term *media* refers to any method for transmitting information between a sender and receiver, but more contemporarily it refers to an instructional technology, such as audiovisual equipment, a web-based tutorial, or a DVD. Instructional methods include techniques such as lectures, discussions, game playing, demonstrations, and so on. Here is an example of an articulated instructional strategy. "First, the students will watch a five-minute video in which a librarian is shown going through a one-on-one consultation with a student in which a research question is being developed. Second, students will go through a fifteen-minute drill-and-practice writing a research question for a sample assignment." This includes two different instructional strategies: an audiovisual presentation and a drill-and-practice immediately afterward that gets the students practicing the skills needed to accomplish the learning outcome.

Table 3-1 is an example of an actual design grid; this is what should come out of the design stage.

Take note that a librarian equipped with a firm knowledge of pedagogy makes it a point to offer a mix of instructional methods, some that incorporate technology and others that do not, that will address the needs of different learners. The selection of drill-and-practice as a secondary instructional method fits in well with a writing class where skills are often developed through repetitive exercises. The completed design grid will feature perhaps three to five specific objectives that the librarian believes will specify how the content will be learned. The librarian will also share the grid with the instructor to obtain feedback in order to make sure the objectives, assessment, and instructional strategies are both feasible and manageable.

TABLE 3-1
Design grid for an information literacy instruction project

Objectives	*Assessment Items*	*Instructional Strategy*
The students will complete an exercise in which they translate research topics into research questions. This will be completed as an assignment for review in class. Students should successfully convert eight of ten topics to acceptable research questions.	Product (written exercise). This is a one-page instrument completed by the student. The research questions completed will be reviewed by a peer faculty member or librarian for completeness and how well they demonstrate a grasp of question preparation.	Drill-and-practice module. The student can repeatedly go through the steps in the process of writing research questions. Rationale: Students need to make a habit out of the process of developing a research question.
Students must select the most appropriate database(s) when given a specific topic or search subject 80 percent of the time.	Multiple choice pre- and post-tests. Within different disciplines, the student will select the most appropriate database from a choice of several databases. Tests can be taken and graded online using course management software.	Tutorial. A static web page using text and screen shots will introduce the student to the spectrum of library databases by discipline. Rationale: This will give the student a self-paced and self-guided method of discovering the significant databases in each discipline covered within the university curriculum.
Students will demonstrate the ability to develop a search strategy for an articulated search question they created in an earlier part of the assignment. Correct search strategies must use at least two synonymous terms and appropriate logical connectors.	Worksheet. The worksheet will have examples and spaces where the student can convert his or her articulated search questions into search strategies. The librarian and instructor will review the worksheet to determine whether the objective was achieved.	Peer analysis. Students will complete the worksheet in teams. They will help each other develop synonymous terms and choose the appropriate logical connectors. Rationale: Worksheets are simple, nonthreatening approaches to getting the student to think about the activity. Peer analysis will help students see that their peers are good sources for assistance with search strategies.

DEVELOPMENT: CREATING THE INSTRUCTIONAL PRODUCT

Now that the librarian has designed the blueprint for the instruction session and related instructional materials, it is time to move into the development phase. Development focuses on the production process for the creation of the instructional product. For example, once the librarian has decided to use a worksheet, it would be created in the development phase, as would any other media needed for the instruction to be implemented. In addition to the worksheet, the pre- and post-tests would be developed, along with any other exercises for use in the instruction activity. As with ADDIE itself, there are many different models for the development phase. Among these many models, there appear to be four phases most often discussed. They are

- Prototype
- Create/Build
- Formative Evaluation
- Revision

Developing prototypes can take on many meanings. If one is simply creating a worksheet, the prototyping process might consist of word processing a rough draft of the sheet. If the developer wanted to take things to the next level, and anticipated that other librarians would be joining the prototyping process, the prototyping activity might escalate to include a set of storyboard-type layouts for what the worksheet activities would look like. If the development team decided, for example, that they wanted to produce a short video or web tutorial to show to the students as part of an instruction session, it might be developed in an even more detailed storyboarding process. The whole point of the prototyping process is to develop models for the instruction product without actually creating a complete and final version. The prototype is a rapidly developed draft, so to speak, that allows the development team to brainstorm and explore multiple ideas before they engage in the actual creation process.

Storyboarding is a part of the prototyping process that would be more necessary for the development of higher-level learning materials. Figures 3-1, 3-2, and 3-3 show three sample storyboards from a prototyping process to develop a web-based tutorial to help students learn how to find library databases and search them. The storyboard process gives the development team a much better idea of what will go into the actual instructional product, and it is much easier to make changes in this stage. You should also note that each storyboard corresponds to a segment of a flowchart. This indicates what part of the instruction product is

Name: InfoLit Team
Client: PhilaU
Fall 2006

Scene Title: Explore database chart for business research

Date of Production: September 15, 2006

Description of Activity

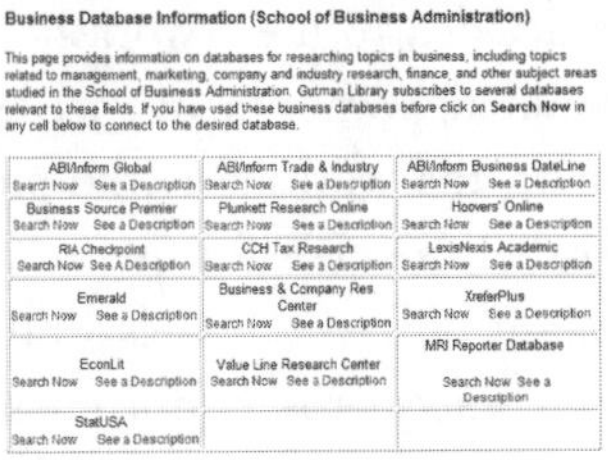

Business Database Information (School of Business Administration)

This page provides information on databases for researching topics in business, including topics related to management, marketing, company and industry research, finance, and other subject areas studied in the School of Business Administration. Gutman Library subscribes to several databases relevant to these fields. If you have used these business databases before click on **Search Now** in any cell below to connect to the desired database.

ABI/Inform Global Search Now See a Description	ABI/Inform Trade & Industry Search Now See a Description	ABI/Inform Business DateLine Search Now See a Description
Business Source Premier Search Now See a Description	Plunkett Research Online Search Now See a Description	Hoovers' Online Search Now See a Description
RIA Checkpoint Search Now See A Description	CCH Tax Research Search Now See a Description	LexisNexis Academic Search Now See a Description
Emerald Search Now See a Description	Business & Company Res Center Search Now See a Description	XreferPlus Search Now See a Description
EconLit Search Now See a Description	Value Line Research Center Search Now See a Description	MRI Reporter Database Search Now See a Description
StatUSA Search Now See a Description		

Capture image of business database chart for this sequence

Action Details/Notes

Narrator instructs learner to review the descriptions of the business databases.

Learner can click on a specific icon to hear a research scenario described with the database solution.

Assessment Module: Incorporate quiz that provides a research scenario and requires learner to choose the correct database to use to conduct the research needed for resolving that scenario.
Flowchart Link 1.9

Flowchart Link: Submenu 1.5, Submenu 1.7, Submenu 1.7

Programming Notes: Will develop multiple research scenarios for each database using anecdotes from SME. Graphic file is dbchart1.jpg. Need to program icon that learner clicks on to go to research scenario.

FIGURE 3-1
Storyboard example no. 1: Database chart

connected to the task analysis. This makes it clear to the development team that each part of the instruction product is based on filling a previously identified learning gap.

The remaining three phases in the development process are fairly straightforward. Once decisions are made about the materials to produce and what media to include in the production stage, the librarian would create the appropriate instructional products. The term *formative evaluation* is phrased as such because it is evaluation that occurs during the forming of the product. The individual developing the product would take opportunities to try it out on members of the target audience to determine whether it is likely to meet the objectives. Professional instructional designers are likely to have a fairly involved formative evaluation process that involves both alpha and beta test phases. Most librarians, at best, will have an opportunity to allow test students to sample the product. This provides an opportunity for revision. The ability to rapidly spot problems and make corrections is an important skill. It requires the ability to identify learning failures. By learning failure we mean that the instruction product is used by students but that they fail to successfully retain the knowledge transferred during the learning

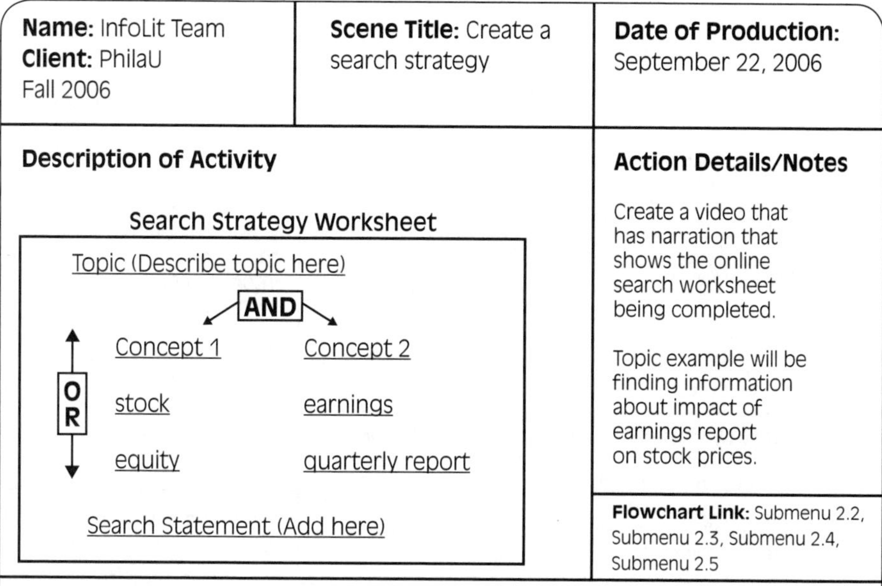

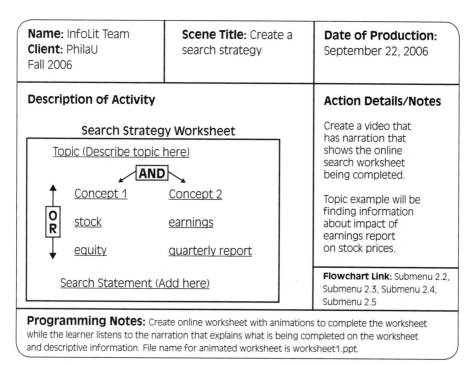

FIGURE 3-2

Storyboard example no. 2: Search strategy worksheet

process. The intended outcome is not achieved. When the developers have sufficiently evaluated what caused the learning failure and made the necessary revisions, it's time to move ahead to implementation.

IMPLEMENTATION: PLANNING FOR THE LAUNCH

Up to this point, the focus of the instructional design process has been planning and testing. It would be easy enough to just put the product into use, but instructional designers are rather methodical, so they usually develop a plan that will help guide the implementation process. The thinking behind the implementation plan is that you want to avoid just releasing the instruction product. The goal is to ensure a successful implementation. This is best achieved by first determining how to create the optimal conditions for a successful launch or implementation. There are four parts to the implementation plan:

- Diffusion
- Training
- Resource Allocation
- Budget

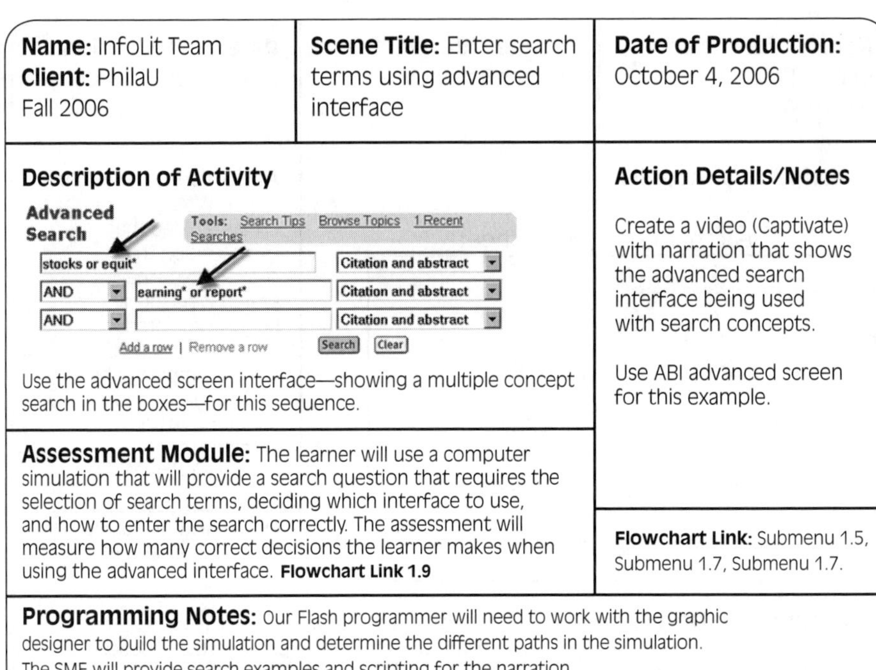

Name: InfoLit Team
Client: PhilaU
Fall 2006

Scene Title: Enter search terms using advanced interface

Date of Production: October 4, 2006

Description of Activity

Use the advanced screen interface—showing a multiple concept search in the boxes—for this sequence.

Action Details/Notes

Create a video (Captivate) with narration that shows the advanced search interface being used with search concepts.

Use ABI advanced screen for this example.

Assessment Module: The learner will use a computer simulation that will provide a search question that requires the selection of search terms, deciding which interface to use, and how to enter the search correctly. The assessment will measure how many correct decisions the learner makes when using the advanced interface. **Flowchart Link 1.9**

Flowchart Link: Submenu 1.5, Submenu 1.7, Submenu 1.7.

Programming Notes: Our Flash programmer will need to work with the graphic designer to build the simulation and determine the different paths in the simulation. The SME will provide search examples and scripting for the narration.

FIGURE 3-3
Storyboard example no. 3: Advanced database search

This may seem like overkill for a library project, but it actually presents an opportunity to carefully think through how to properly implement the instruction product. It has the hallmarks of design thinking because it requires a thoughtful and deliberate process that guides the introduction of this new resource for user education.

The idea behind diffusion is simply to set the stage for the adoption of the instruction product. Why bother to create an instruction product if not to see it being used? In the instructional design world, diffusion tends to apply more to new innovations or designs that others need to adopt. If diffused properly, the innovation spreads through the adoption process. In the academic library world, we simply want our students and faculty to adopt our instruction methods. Still, there are points to remember in achieving better diffusion, such as avoiding extreme complexity, seeking compatibility with existing products, and having some communication strategies for sharing information about the instructional product.

Training means that anyone who will be working with the new instruction product and related materials will need the right skills to successfully use them with the learners. This means a bit of advanced preparation and answering some questions. How much training will be needed? Who will organize the training sessions and conduct them? Could anyone outside the library (e.g., faculty) take advantage of the training? Once some of these questions have been answered, the designers can develop an appropriate training session. Resource allocation connects to both diffusion and training. It asks what funding is needed to ensure a successful implementation. This may not apply to an instruction product developed for a single course, but it certainly might for a campuswide initiative, such as the implementation of an information literacy initiative or a learning module that all students will be required to use.

Here are some final points on creating the right conditions for a successful implementation in an academic setting:

- Obtain support from faculty and administrators for a new instruction product
- Convince faculty and administrators of the instruction product's value
- Ensure that support structures required by the instruction product are in place
- Ensure that any additional resources needed to implement the instruction product are available
- Identify librarians and faculty who will be using the instruction product and provide proper training and support

SUMMATIVE EVALUATION: DID WE GET IT RIGHT?

The final phase of ADDIE is one of the most important ones because it determines the overall success of the instructional product. In the final analysis, what matters is whether the learning gap was eliminated by the instruction product. As is the case with the growing focus on accountability in higher education, blended librarians must demonstrate that the design of their services and resources successfully furthers the institutional goal of helping students to achieve learning outcomes. The best way to do that is to have clearly identified objectives at the beginning of a project that allow for effective assessment at the end of the project. One of the failings of many library projects is that they are not influenced by a design process such as ADDIE. Since they are developed with no clear objectives in mind, there is no way to determine if the desired results were truly achieved. One of the benefits of following an ADDIE design process is that developing clear objectives is an integral part of the design phase.

Similarly, evaluation is an integral part of ADDIE. However, it is a somewhat different form of evaluation than the one that occurred during the development phase. In ADDIE the final phase of evaluation is referred to more specifically as summative evaluation. The goal in this phase is initially to collect, analyze, and report findings on the "summed" effect of the instruction product. Ultimately the goal is to answer the question, "Have we solved the problem?" and identify revisions that could help to improve the instruction product. Summative evaluation often takes place a few weeks or months after implementation. It will take some passage of time before objectives related to correcting the learning gap can be properly assessed. It is unlikely that students would demonstrate a difference as a result of the instruction product immediately after their initial exposure.

Any number of factors could potentially be included in the summative phase. These could include costs, impact on the organization, how well the instruction product was accepted by the learners and instructors, and a host of other possibilities. Whatever factors the designers decide to include in their evaluation, they will typically fit them into three main areas: effectiveness, efficiency, and benefits. Effectiveness focuses on the instruction and asks if students were able to achieve the objectives for learning. There should be some decisions made in advance about how effectiveness will be determined. It could involve testing, portfolio reviews, or analysis of data from the student reports. Efficiency examines the actual process to develop and implement the instruction. This could include the time it took to develop and deliver, the impact on faculty, or other issues related to the degree of effort that was needed to implement the instruction product. Deriving the benefits of the program is something of a mix of efficiency and effectiveness but seeks to determine if the objectives were achieved in a way that benefited the organization. That is, perhaps the objectives were achieved to satisfaction but at too high a cost to justify in the future. Ideally, they would be achieved at a cost that is deemed acceptable.

The final aspect of summative evaluation may be optional for a library project but could be of use in sharing the results of the instructional design process with colleagues and faculty. Dissemination is the process of creating a report for the project and distributing it to the parties involved in the instruction. It would probably be a good idea to decide at the beginning of the project if a report is needed or desirable. If it is, then it is easier to collect and organize data for the report as it progresses. Trying to gather all the report data at the end is time-consuming, something is bound to be missed, and is generally less effective. Many instructional design texts, including that of Seels and Glasgow (1998), include lists of what sorts of questions should be addressed in a final report. Owing to their time constraints, academic librarians might wish to just provide an overview of each phase of ADDIE and make recommendations for broad changes, or perhaps just tweaking that would correct minor faults. Though not necessary, dissemination can be a useful part of this process.

BLAAM: AN INSTRUCTIONAL DESIGN MODEL FOR BLENDED LIBRARIANS

Clearly, professional instructional designers would spend considerable time on all ADDIE phases. A project to develop a digital instruction product consisting of multiple instruction modules can realistically take many months, hundreds of hours of labor, and thousands of dollars. TILT was provided as an earlier example of just such an instruction product. It took roughly three years to complete. TILT is certainly an impressive and effective way to eliminate some learning gaps, but in reality how many individual academic libraries could develop such a tutorial? (Fortunately, TILT can be freely acquired and adapted by other libraries.) The time, staff, and money needed to conduct full-scale instructional design processes each time a new instructional innovation is contemplated are luxuries that most academic libraries are hardly able to afford. Does this mean that instructional design is beyond the scope of academic librarians and should therefore be ignored? We believe the answer is no.

We instead advocate a blended librarian's approach to ADDIE that would better meet the needs of resource-constrained librarians. Recall that ADDIE is a generic model of instructional systems design. We would hardly be the first to adapt ADDIE to a specific situation or environment. Our model will condense ADDIE into the essential steps for design that complement the resource base of most academic libraries. If the institution has instructional designers on staff and they can be involved in the project, then the blended librarians model can be expanded to include more elements of the comprehensive ADDIE process. We call our model the Blended Librarians Adapted ADDIE Model (BLAAM). The following description of the phases in developing an instruction product for a faculty member's research assignment provides insight into the application of BLAAM.

The first phase in BLAAM is Assess. It is critical to understand the needs of the learners when developing an instruction product to fill a learning gap. However, BLAAM simply suggests that librarians take some time to assess the learning situation in order to better understand what the faculty member's learning outcomes are and where the students are deficient in achieving them. This stage should require only two actions. First, discuss the learning situation and outcomes with the faculty member, and second, conduct an informal needs assessment of the students. The assessment can take the form of a quick survey, possibly using the tools integrated into courseware systems. As a result of these information-gathering functions, the production of a simple problem statement should be possible. The task analysis and other elements that are a part of ADDIE's analysis phase are eliminated. So the goal of Assess is to develop a problem statement that identifies the learning gap. An example of a problem statement would be: "Several semesters of final paper projects in L371 indicate that students rely too heavily on free Internet resources, that they are unfamiliar with the top essential databases in their discipline, and that they lack the necessary skills to properly cite resources." Keep the problem statement simple but direct.

The second phase of BLAAM is Objectives. The design phase of ADDIE contains some important processes, but perhaps the essential one for academic librarians is the establishment of clear, measurable objectives. The goal of this phase is to establish outcomes that make it clear to all involved in the process what the instruction product or session needs to accomplish in order to be determined successful. In the event the project is unsuccessful to any degree, it may be necessary to revise some of the outcomes or determine where the failures occurred in the full BLAAM process. The process of writing objectives is no different; it can still be guided by the A-B-C-D method. But to save time, the objective will include a statement about both assessment and instruction method. We acknowledge this is a significant compression of the objectives process, but our rationale is that without sacrificing certain parts of the ADDIE model, most academic librarians will likely entirely disregard this critical step in the instructional design process. So to our way of thinking, some objective development is better than none, and we hope our suggested methods will still result in the creation of achievable and measurable objectives. The creation of a design grid should be considered optional. Create one only if time allows. Also, rather than writing a set of five or more objectives, the goal should be to focus on three core objectives for any instruction project. For this project the objectives would include

1. Students in L371 will demonstrate the balanced use of information resources in their research projects to include equal numbers of references from free Internet and commercial library sources as evidenced by their bibliographies; the students will be provided with a web-based template for completing the research that will guide them to specific resources representing the free Internet and library databases.
2. Students in L371 will work through a video screencast tutorial that introduces them to two key library databases in their discipline; at the completion of the screencast, the students will take a feedback quiz in their courseware site that will let them know if they are ready to search the library's databases in their discipline.
3. Students in L371 will learn how to cite their work using a major citation format (as specified by the instructor) and will need to demonstrate the quality of their citations in their research paper bibliography. Students

will learn how to use the library's citation-formatting tools in a hands-on session in the computer lab during their regular class time.

The third phase of BLAAM is, just as in ADDIE, Develop. The difference is that in BLAAM it is compressed for a less intensive development process than one would experience with a real instructional design team. The one area most abbreviated is prototyping. While it is important to invest time in testing models prior to the actual creation of the instruction product, at best we would expect an outline, draft, mock-up, or other document that would serve as a rough draft of the product. While storyboards can take days or weeks to produce, this part of the process would require just a few hours needed to draft a plan for the instruction product. Sharing the plan with colleagues or the instructor would provide early feedback in the development process. Once satisfied with the plan, the next step would be the actual creation of whatever documents, multimedia, or materials are needed to conduct the instruction session. With low budgets and short time frames, the instruction materials developed in the BLAAM approach would be simple in nature, with a minimum of features and advanced technology. Formative evaluation would need to be replaced or omitted in BLAAM. There might be an opportunity for some formal evaluation of the instruction product, but in all likelihood it would need to be done quickly, perhaps by a brief survey disseminated to students at the end of the instruction session.

The fourth phase of BLAAM is Deliver. Without much time or fanfare for disseminating information about the instruction product, the librarian delivers the instruction product or session he or she has developed. The intent of ADDIE's implementation phase is to create the conditions for the instruction product's success. It is easy to understand the importance of going to great lengths to achieve diffusion when the product has taken months, many hours of labor, and thousands of dollars to produce. Under such conditions, every precaution to eliminate the chance of failure should be taken. But in a library instruction setting, the stakes are far lower. Granted, we want our instruction products or services to succeed, but if they fail to accomplish what they were designed for, the loss in time and resources is minimal, and we have opportunities to try again. If an instructional design firm's products fail, they stand to lose clients and go out of business, so it's to their advantage to take implementation quite seriously. Librarians practicing BLAAM should focus on getting their instruction product ready for use, and this means emphasizing training. Make sure that anyone who needs to use the instruction product is fully familiar with its features and operation. The one place that even we would like to prevent failure is in the classroom with our students and faculty. Training and good preparation in the Deliver phase should strengthen the chances for success.

The fifth and final phase of BLAAM is Measure. The goal is to refer back to the stated objectives or outcomes and measure the degree to which they were achieved during the instruction process. If the objectives were designed thoughtfully, it should indicate how they are measured. For example, if the students were developing bibliographies to demonstrate the ability to properly cite materials, measurement needs to include a review of the bibliographies to determine the extent to which the instruction product accounted for student learning. Other methods could include a brief evaluation form distributed to students after the instruction to gain their assessment of the instruction product or session, or could involve having students complete the post-test designed for this instruction. In this era of accountability and emphasis on achieving stated outcomes, measurement is a critical phase of BLAAM. It would be similar to the summative evaluation phase of ADDIE, but the time period between the delivery and evaluation stages would be much shorter, and by comparison the measurement methods would be far less elaborate. But the goal should be to provide evidence that learning occurred or to gather the necessary information to make needed enhancements to the instruction product for the next time it is delivered.

To summarize, here is a comparison of the BLAAM and ADDIE models:

BLAAM	**ADDIE**
Assess	Analyze
Objectives	Design
Develop	Develop
Deliver	Implement
Measure	Evaluate

We hope that academic librarians will take advantage of these models to better incorporate design thinking into their instruction products. But the two models are not mutually exclusive. In identifying and resolving information gaps, each librarian should determine which elements of each model best fit his or her own culture and situation. It may be that in a particular situation, starting with BLAAM's abbreviated assessment and objective-writing process is the best way to begin, but that it makes sense to spend more time on a thorough prototyping process. Design is largely situational, and what works in one environment may not work in another. We recommend that these two models be viewed as a menu from which different methods can be adapted to unique learning problems and the solutions that will eliminate those problems.

CONCLUSION

If you have been wondering about the ways academic librarians can incorporate design thinking into their practice, we hope this chapter provides a better picture of how that can happen. Instructional design is a process that incorporates and gives structure to the principles of design thinking. You can clearly see how ADDIE or BLAAM forces a librarian to be far more thoughtful and intentional about the design, development, and implementation of instruction products. But the concepts behind instructional design can also be applied to other areas of our work. Beyond instruction, we may wish to apply instructional design practices to the development of a new service to improve communications with the user community. They could be applied to the acquisition, implementation, and delivery of a new technology. The essence of instructional design is to engage in a structured process by which we and our academic colleagues can determine if new services and innovations are truly worthwhile, and if so, we can collaboratively set a path to acquire and implement them in a way that establishes the conditions for success. When you think about this it makes great sense. Understanding instructional design and then integrating it into one's skill set, which is at the core of blended librarianship, has infinite advantages over the haphazard and ambiguous methods of innovation and implementation that our profession has practiced in the past.

TOPICS FOR FURTHER DISCUSSION

At your library, has any previous effort to use an instructional design approach been made? If so, how did it help to improve the quality of instruction or services? If not, what specific instruction or services do you think it can help to improve?

Do you think BLAAM is still realistic for many frontline practitioners? In what ways do you think you could implement it in your work? Are there parts of BLAAM that might be of more value than others in your work?

What challenges might you face in your library if you seek to get either administrative or colleague support for instituting instructional design processes when new instruction or services are being planned?

ADDITIONAL RESOURCES

Dick, Walter, Lou Carey, and James O. Carey. 2004. *The Systematic Design of Instruction.* 6th ed. Boston: Allyn and Bacon.

Encyclopedia of Educational Technology. http://coe.sdsu.edu/eet/Admin/index.htm (conduct a search on "ADDIE" or "instructional design").

Gagne, Robert Mills. 2005. *Principles of Instructional Design.* Belmont, Calif.: Thomson/Wadsworth.

Idaho State University, College of Education. "ADDIE Resource Page." http://ed.isu.edu/addie/.

Introduction to Instructional Systems Design. http://www.nwlink.com/~donclark/hrd/sat1.html.

University of Colorado at Denver, School of Education. "Instructional Design Models." http://carbon.cudenver.edu/~mryder/itc_data/idmodels.html.

Wikipedia entry on ADDIE. http://en.wikipedia.org/wiki/ADDIE.

4 What's in It for Them?

Furthering Campus Collaboration through Design Thinking

Great discoveries and improvements invariably involve the cooperation of many minds. —Alexander Graham Bell

OBJECTIVES

1. Familiarize the reader with general issues and concerns related to collaborative efforts with faculty and other academic support professionals.
2. Identify techniques to open up more opportunities for collaboration.
3. Present case studies of collaborative activities between librarians, faculty, and other academic support professionals that work.

MAKING THE CASE FOR WIIFM

If we envision any one area where we would like to see design thinking making a difference in academic librarianship, it is in facilitating better collaborative relations on campus. In our workshops and consultations, perhaps the most frequent point of frustration we hear about from our library colleagues is their inability to achieve fruitful collaboration with their faculty colleagues. Faculty collaboration is the subject of dozens of articles and at least one book in the library literature, all posing or exploring the same question: how do we successfully engage in truly productive collaborative relations with our faculty? As blended librarians we certainly want to enhance our collaborative activity with our faculty, but we think it's equally important to establish collaborative relationships with others beyond the faculty. To achieve our outcomes we must also work collaboratively with our fellow academic support professionals. Academic librarians have traditionally collaborated with colleagues from the campus writing program staff and the teaching and learning center. But now we must reach out and establish relationships with newer colleagues who include instructional designers, instructional technologists, and information technologists.

While we believe that design thinking can help academic librarians to accomplish any number of beneficial services, design thinking alone will not improve or increase the opportunities for collaborative activity between librarians and faculty. So what value can design have in this instance? To answer that question we point to WIIFM, which stands for "What's in it for me?" Some faculty are eager to collaborate with academic librarians and need to do so because they believe it benefits their students. But the vast majority of faculty are in need of further justification for spending time and effort on collaboration. To facilitate collaboration, we believe it is important to first demonstrate to faculty why there is something in it for them. We will explore this, and how design thinking can help academic librarians turn WIIFM from a barrier into a catalyst for collaboration, in this chapter.

Why is librarian-faculty collaboration of such great importance? On one level, academic librarians have a subconscious chip on their shoulder about playing a subservient role to faculty in the higher education enterprise. The debate about tenure for academic librarians is, to an extent, about achieving parity with faculty. If librarians had equal status with faculty, the rationale goes, faculty would be far more likely to view their library colleagues as academic partners and be open to collaborating with them. On a deeper level, we find a much more important reason to collaborate with our faculty. Our faculty colleagues can help us communicate our message about the importance of information literacy skills for students, educate students on the value of using library services and resources, and integrate the academic librarian as a learning partner in physical and virtual courses. As blended librarians we can help them to make this happen.

WHO INFLUENCES COLLEGE STUDENTS?

We now have more evidence about the vastly influential role that faculty have on students when it comes to library resources and research. In 2006 OCLC published *College Students' Perceptions of Libraries and Information Resources,* a subset of a larger, similar study published the previous year (DeRosa et al. 2006). The report offers valuable insight into the role that academic librarians play in shaping the information-gathering skills of college students. Two findings are of particular significance to our understanding of the importance of collaboration with faculty. The first is how students answered the question, "How do you learn about electronic information sources?" (See figure 4-1.) The top-ranked source is "friend," but the second-ranked personal source that students consult to learn about electronic information sources is "teacher." Farther down on the list "librarian" is mentioned. But it is clear that students spend more time with faculty, and

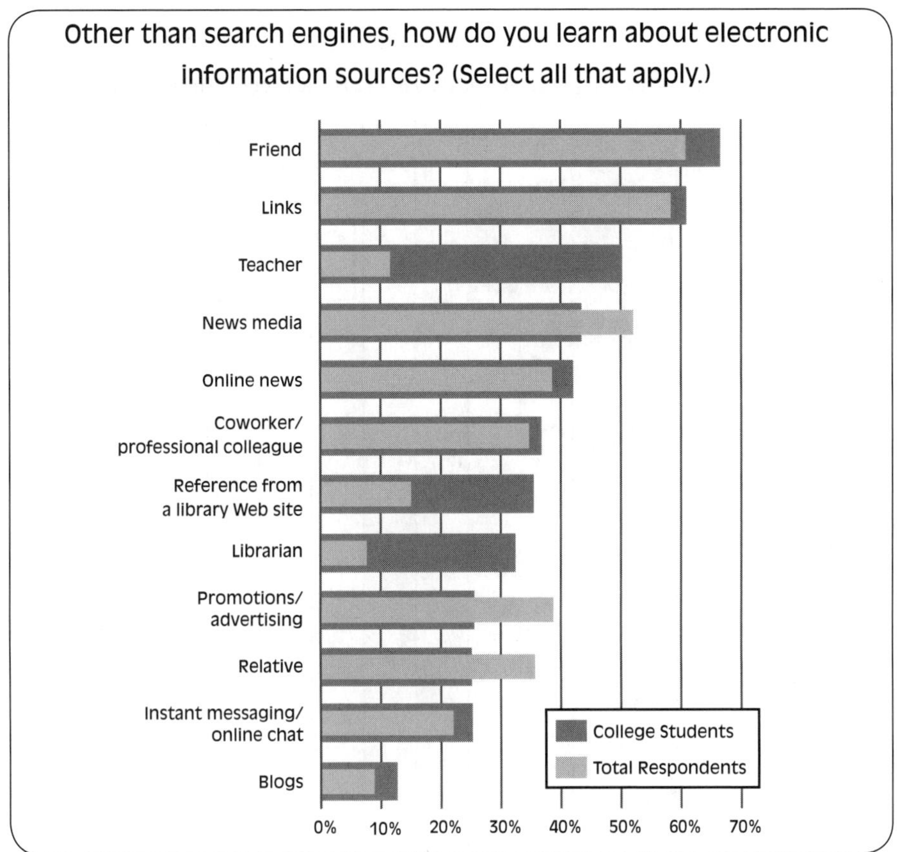

FIGURE 4-1

How students learn about electronic resources

Source: DeRosa et al. 2006, 1-9. © 2006 OCLC Online Computer Library Center, Inc. Used with permission.

this time presents great opportunities for faculty to encourage students to use the library's electronic sources. If academic librarians want students to learn more about library services and resources, the path to success goes directly through the classroom.

The second finding is also quite revealing in that it reinforces what we suspected from anecdotal evidence about the impact librarians have on students versus the influential role of faculty members (see figure 4-2). When asked, "Who or what is that trusted source you most typically use?" to validate the accuracy or reliability of information, college students ranked "teacher/professor" as their first choice (45 percent of respondents chose faculty). "Librarian" was much farther

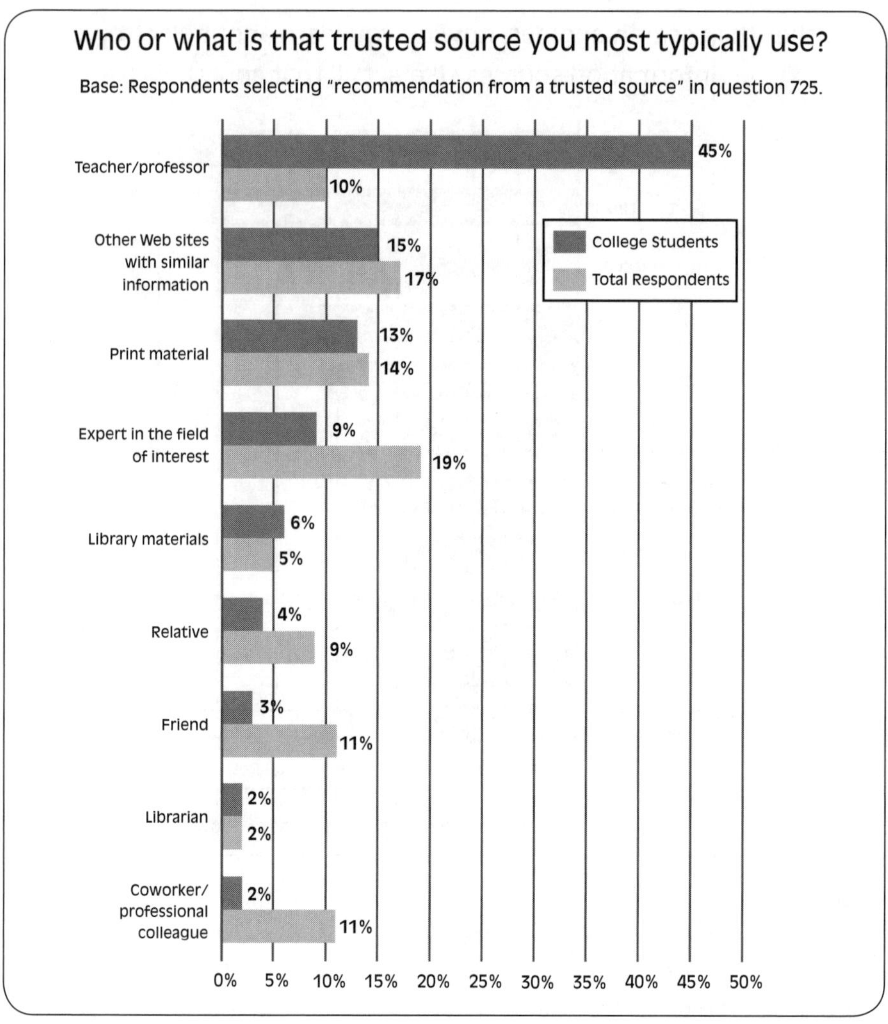

FIGURE 4-2

Students' trusted resources for validating information

Source: DeRosa et al. 2006, 3-11. © 2006 OCLC Online Computer Library Center, Inc. Used with permission.

down the list, even lower than "friend" or "relative," with just 2 percent of respondents indicating they would seek out a librarian as a trusted source for validating information. Either we must do much more to build college students' confidence in librarians or we must identify and develop better ways to collaborate with faculty so we can encourage them to spread the word about academic librarians as valued guides to the information maze.

WHY IS COLLABORATION WITH FACULTY AN ELUSIVE GOAL?

Academic librarians often ask, and rightfully so, why faculty are reluctant to collaborate with them. While there is a reasonable amount of literature that documents librarian-faculty collaboration and provides evidence that not all faculty are opposed to collaboration with librarians, there is little research that documents or seeks to understand the barriers to collaboration. At least one study did attempt to analyze the librarian-faculty relationship in search of answers. One of the best-known observations in library literature about faculty collaboration with librarians is found in an article titled "A Report on Librarian-Faculty Relations from a Sociological Perspective" (Christiansen, Stombler, and Thaxton 2004).

This is an important article for understanding the challenges in achieving collaboration with faculty because, as the article states, there "is an asymmetrical disconnection that exists between librarians and faculty . . . the two groups are generally separated." Academic librarians are often left wondering why faculty are reluctant to collaborate on assignment design, for example, when we have such great "potential for interaction, collaboration, and shared interests in quality teaching and research." But the reality, as this article elaborates, is that while librarians consider the disconnect to be problematic, "faculty acknowledge the disconnect but they do not consider it to be problematic." So where we see lack of collaboration as a problem, faculty consider it the norm for an academic institution. And where we see ourselves as having a role in or wanting to be more integrated into the teaching and learning process, the article's most disturbing conclusion is that "in the eyes of the faculty, librarians do not appear to play a central role in faculty teaching."

As stated above, while there are certainly challenges to achieving collaboration with faculty, it is possible. Those seeking to learn from the best practices of other academic libraries would do well to read Raspa and Ward's book, *The Collaborative Imperative: Librarians and Faculty Working Together in the Information Universe* (2000). It offers several case studies that provide evidence that good collaborative programs exist and that many of them are rooted in the delivery of information literacy education to students. "Each of the programs selected for study . . . demonstrates the fact that interest among the academic library community in collaborative approaches to instruction and promoting information literacy skills across the entire university community comes at a good time" (Walter 2000). Some of the exemplary programs highlighted in Raspa and Ward include

> At Earlham College, instruction occurs in response to an assignment developed in collaboration between a teaching faculty member and a librarian.

Seventy to eighty percent of Earlham faculty incorporate library instruction into at least one course taught.

At Indiana University–Purdue University at Indianapolis, librarians serve on collaborative teams to deliver instruction within a one-credit required course. Coupled with a departmental faculty member, and with support from student advisors and computer technologists, the librarians conduct several sessions of the course per semester.

At Evergreen State College, since 1977, librarians have had the opportunity to participate in a rotation program with classroom faculty that brings librarians into the classroom and members of the classroom faculty into the library. Information literacy instruction at Evergreen became increasingly collaborative as librarians and faculty both integrated it into the coursework.

At the University of Washington, the UWIRED program places a major emphasis on faculty and librarian development and collaboration. UWIRED seeks to foster the integration of technology into the teaching and learning process. It brought faculty and librarians together through joint technology training and stimulated the growth of information literacy programming.

At the Virginia Polytechnic Institute and State University, an outreach librarian position was created, someone dedicated to proactive outreach activities aimed at faculty, in order to raise the status and recognition that librarians receive from faculty members. By creating physical offices for librarians in the area of the faculty offices, the librarians were able to engage in many different acts of collaborative enterprise, from the development of resource guides and web pages to more traditional instruction activity.

Although the literature reports such examples as these to remind us that faculty collaboration is certainly possible, these programs are more the exception than the rule. In the cases of Earlham and Evergreen colleges, these are fairly small academic institutions with a significant teaching culture, and they are unusual in that their campuses embrace collaboration between librarians and faculty. The research university examples are perhaps better in that they symbolize the value of collaboration even when it may not be a campuswide phenomenon. Furthermore, in most of these examples the collaborative activity is information literacy, and while that is important, our profession needs to create other forms and methods for enhancing collaboration with faculty and other academic support professions (the latter are barely noted in these case studies).

At least one survey identified library instruction as the type of collaboration mentioned most frequently by librarians. While it would be unfair to describe library instruction as the low-hanging fruit of librarian-faculty collaboration, there are other forms of collaboration that can occur but do so far less frequently. Examples of less frequently observed collaboration include team teaching, guest lecturing, cobuilding areas of a courseware site, cosponsoring a joint campus event or conference, and the joint creation of digital learning materials or joint course development (Jeffries 2000). These less traditional forms of collaboration, while not necessarily more meaningful for furthering student learning outcomes, are good examples of what blended librarians refer to as "creating the connections." Given the challenges of achieving librarian-faculty collaboration on many campuses, and acknowledging that often librarian expectations for it are set too high, we advance the idea of targeting some intermediate approaches that could lead to fuller forms of collaboration, especially those that directly result in the achievement of student learning outcomes. The key to identifying and developing those types of activities that contribute to the creation of connections is to grasp and leverage WIIFM.

USING WIIFM TO OUR ADVANTAGE

As academic librarians, our primary interest in collaborating with faculty is to further our information literacy mission by encouraging faculty to develop an assignment with us, or allow us to provide an instruction session to a class, or possibly partner with us to develop an intricate information literacy project. As blended librarians, our goals for faculty collaboration are somewhat more focused. While we still hope to achieve mutual goals with faculty for information literacy, much of our effort could be described as working to create the connections that lead to ongoing and deeper collaboration. One way to facilitate those connections is by doing something for faculty that, put simply, helps them save time, gain efficiency, or enables them to effectively use a new technology. We refer to this as "meeting the WIIFM factor."

As important or necessary as we may think our services and resources are, they may actually be of little interest to faculty. It's not that faculty choose to intentionally ignore the value of the library's resources and services to the teaching and learning process, but rather they often lack the time needed to invest in learning some of our new research techniques. For faculty, learning the research techniques associated with the myriad of library electronic databases is equivalent to adopting new technologies. One of the greatest barriers to faculty adopting new technologies is lack of time. Robert DeSieno (1995) sums up faculty's negative feelings toward adopting new technologies, stating that "digital technology requires too much time and effort, supplies too many distractions, and yields too little value for the investment." With responsibilities for multiple courses, many students, research activities, committee duties, and more, how can faculty find the time to learn about and use our resources as well as design instructional opportunities for students to use them creatively? If there was a way to convince faculty that it would save time to learn about and integrate the library's resources into their course methods and help them to gain new efficiencies while providing instructional advantages for their students, then they might be more open to collaborations with librarians. It is up to academic librarians to design the methods and instructional products that will meet the WIIFM factor.

Chickering and Gamson (1987) identified seven principles for good teaching and instruction. These principles suggested to faculty that their teaching would improve if they did such things as encourage contact between themselves and students, develop reciprocity and cooperation among students, use active learning techniques, provide prompt feedback, emphasize time spent on tasks, communicate high expectations, and respect diverse talents and ways of learning. The principle that resonates most strongly with blended librarians is time on task. Chickering and Gamson said that effective faculty needed to ensure that students spent adequate amounts of time on learning tasks. Additionally, they advised faculty to achieve efficiencies in the organization of the course and instructional methods that would save their own time and the time of their students. The seven principles were later updated by Chickering and Ehrmann (1996) to reflect the availability of new technologies for learning. Again, the authors recommended that new technologies be leveraged to save time on task.

How might a technology be used to create more time on task while clearly demonstrating to faculty that it can achieve something that is important to them as educators or researchers? At one of the author's own institutions, he routinely encountered faculty members who complained about their students' lack of knowledge about current events in the world at large and within their own disciplines. Given that students are readily distracted by all forms of electronic communication and entertainment, it's no surprise they may rarely read a national newspaper or relevant trade publication. When the author heard this exact complaint from a faculty colleague to whom he had provided research and courseware assistance on several previous occasions, he saw the opportunity to make a collaborative connection. The instructor's concern was about certain area studies courses she taught where the students were painfully unaware of any current news coming out of several European countries.

Since the author had previously provided some assistance with this faculty member's courseware site, he suggested using RSS (Real Simple Syndication) technology to capture mainstream media news and direct it onto her courseware site's announcements page. After explaining some basics about RSS technology and what it makes possible, the author and faculty member met to discuss how this might work. At this meeting the author demonstrated how an RSS feed could be fed into a courseware site on the Blackboard system. At the meeting they mutually determined that the *Financial Times* of London would serve as a good media source for this project. The *Financial Times* offers many feeds for different countries and regions of the world, and upon reviewing them the faculty member asked the author to deliver several of them into her course. Within a day the author had created five news feeds that would be integrated into the announcements page of the faculty member's courseware site. This meant that whenever the students entered the faculty member's courseware site, the first thing they would see would be the latest news headlines from the relevant sections of the *Financial Times.* This application of technology made it possible for the faculty member to accomplish something she valued: getting her students more exposed to current European news, and this motivated her to collaborate because it allowed her to further her goals for the course. While it took some time to learn more about RSS and how it could be integrated into the courseware site, there was something in it for her.

Although it may sound cynical to suggest that the only way librarians can achieve collaboration with faculty is to give them something they need in order to get something we want, this is really about taking needed steps to develop a more symbiotic relationship. We are helping faculty, and they are getting the help they need. As blended librarians, our strategy for creating the connections that lead to collaboration with faculty should focus on time on task and ways in which we can help faculty to achieve greater efficiencies for themselves and their students. When we are able to offer something to faculty that clearly demonstrates there is something in it for them, we are far more likely to advance our goal of furthering collaborative activity than if we expect faculty to collaborate with us simply because we think they should. Chapters 5, 6, and 7 of this book will offer examples of tools and techniques that blended librarians can develop that we believe meet the WIIFM factor. These examples are ones that we and blended librarian colleagues have successfully used to help faculty improve time on task.

COLLABORATION WITH OTHER ACADEMIC PARTNERS

When it comes to collaboration, the academic librarian's focus is largely on faculty. That makes good sense because our actual or desired relationship with faculty is what best furthers our objective of encouraging high-quality student research. But to focus our collaborative energy solely on faculty may cause academic librarians to miss out on other avenues to engage faculty in collaborative ventures. In particular, we may do well to advance our cause through collaboration with our fellow academic support professionals. This includes familiar colleagues such as teaching and writing center professionals, but we also advocate getting to know some colleagues who are less traditional partners. In this category we would include educational technologists, instructional designers, and instructional technologists. These professionals may be members of an information technology or academic technology unit, but every institution is unique, and there may be variations on this standard organizational structure.

As blended librarians we also advocate that academic librarians should themselves be acquiring instructional design and technology skills. However, to do so does not eliminate the value of collaboration with our professional colleagues who work in these areas. In fact, learning more about their skills, tools, techniques, and jargon can only help to promote better communication and intradepartmental cooperation. There are other benefits as well. The more time spent with instructional designers and technologists, the more likely it is that a blended librarian will increase his or her own knowledge base in these skill areas. It is always best to learn from the experts.

Collaboration between academic librarians and instructional designers and technologists can lead to fruitful outcomes. In the previous chapter we discussed ADDIE and the implications of delving into a full-fledged instructional design process. Clearly, academic librarians could benefit from the expertise of an instructional designer in planning the design of a new instructional product. It may even be that the designer would be willing to participate in the design process, perhaps by assisting with developing an assessment or prototyping the instruction product. Just as academic librarians believe their specialized skills are assets to others in their institutions, they too need to realize when it is more sensible to seek out the aid of more experienced colleagues. Courseware is another good example. In most higher education institutions, a department other than the academic library is responsible for the administration of the courseware system. Therefore, in order to further our goals of integrating the library into faculty courses on the system, we need to build bridges with the educational technologists who manage the courseware. Creating these connections can indeed further the ultimate goal of creating connections with faculty.

How can academic librarians begin to engage in collaborative partnerships with instructional designers and technologists? Some of the same suggestions provided in Raspa and Ward for how to better facilitate collaboration with faculty can also be applied to our academic technology colleagues. These suggestions include things such as taking an interest in their work, reading their literature to familiarize yourself with their contemporary professional issues and jargon, offering to take them to lunch, inviting them to a staff meeting or getting yourself invited to their staff meeting, and creating similar opportunities for interaction. These are all good ideas, but academic librarians may also wish to create those initial connections with a more project-based approach. Our experience is that instructional designers and technologists are hands-on folks, and they like the challenge of an actual project. Good possibilities include seeking advice for a new informational or instructional tutorial, requesting assistance with an ADDIE or BLAAM plan for an upcoming project, or asking for recommendations on how to design a better web page or a library resource page in a courseware site. We have found that these types of projects will better whet the appetite of our academic technology colleagues. We urge readers of this book to add to their campus collaborative relationships those of their colleagues in instructional design and technology.

CASE STUDIES

The following are some case studies that we believe present outstanding efforts to create programs between librarians, faculty, and instructional designers that demonstrate the value of collaboration.

Team Teaching with Faculty: A Rich and Rewarding Experience

CONTRIBUTED BY SUSAN WHYTE, LIBRARY DIRECTOR, LINFIELD COLLEGE

In the spring of 1995, a faculty member from the Mass Communication Department approached me about a new course, Information Gathering, that he was developing as the introduction to the Mass Communication major. Outside of some informal interaction, this professor and I were mostly strangers working at the same institution. I had some previous team-teaching experience and knew how rewarding teaching library research was over the course of a semester-long course. I liked being a teaching librarian whose classroom role expanded beyond bibliographic instruction. In short, I was hungry for content and depth, and my faculty colleague needed someone to teach the library research part of the course. However, initially, my colleague did not see this as a team-taught course. It was his course, and I was going to help him with it. He owned the course. I was useful for my deep knowledge about searching databases.

So, in the fall of 1995, I found myself sitting in on the class three mornings a week, looking to discover the best way to integrate myself into this course.

I gradually contributed more and more to each class session, and the integration process developed over the first year. In this class each student would perform an in-depth, personalized research assignment. The course's final project required the inclusion of books, general periodical articles, scholarly articles, web pages, and interviews with three human experts. The class was writing and research intensive, and we rarely lectured. Instead, the class more resembled a lab experience with abundant hands-on work, close examination of the processes of searching, discovering, writing, thinking, and in the end producing a document of more depth and authority than one would normally find in a sophomore-level course.

Students told us this was the first and sometimes the only course in their career at Linfield where they were allowed to think on their own. They discovered how to learn. We two faculty also learned how to learn as each student probed a different topic area. Emphasis in the course was as much on authority and veracity of sources as on the search process. The course was intense and quickly became known as Information Hell. We taught this course from the fall of 1995 until the fall of 2002, when I had to take a year off in order to lead the design and building of a new library at the college.

In the spring of 2003, my colleague retired, and I thought that my involvement with the class would end as well. We had honed our teaching together, had reached a wonderful level of repartee in class, and had gone through the predictable lows when we thought that the students would never get it, to the highs when so many of them were amazed that they could talk about their research in a coherent manner. He and I grew to treasure our teaching together. He let go of the control of the class early on in our relationship. I grew to trust myself as a teacher. We shared the authority of the teaching/learning experience with the students. We remain deep friends.

In the fall of 2003, the new faculty member in the department hired to teach this course approached me but asked that I provide only library instruction sessions. He, as was his right, re-created the class in his own vision. I needed to let go of my ownership of the class and work to reestablish my prior collaborative role. As the focus of the course changed, the research projects became, for the most part, less personal and harder to comprehend as some students plunged into unfamiliar worlds. Government document research was more significant in the new course, and it challenged the students. There were more preliminary assignments, citing was more strictly interpreted, and grading was more stringent. I was not immediately accepted as a teaching colleague or an equal in the classroom.

But the relationship gradually improved. Within one year I was attending each class session. I began to provide advice on certain students I encountered outside the class. I progressed to the point of reading each assignment and working with the faculty member on grades, but the relationship of collaboration has yet to reach its prior state. I understand now that collaboration or team teaching requires true compatibility. It also requires relentless team building, good listening, flexibility, and a good sense of humor. More important, it requires faculty to relinquish some control of the classroom. For some faculty this is not possible, but it need not create a barrier to the librarian's role as classroom teacher and academic partner.

Fostering Collaborations through a Faculty Learning Community Experience

CONTRIBUTED BY MICHAEL HOWSER, INFORMATION LITERACY COORDINATOR, AND CYNTHIA MADER, ASSISTANT HEAD SCIENCE LIBRARIAN, BRILL SCIENCE LIBRARY, MIAMI UNIVERSITY

With the vast amount of information accessible at students' fingertips today, the question arises as to why the quality of student research seems to be declining. To develop a strategy to counteract this decline requires a new approach, one that involves faculty-librarian collaborations to infuse information literacy concepts within courses, assignments, and disciplines. Through this team approach, we can foster the development of students as lifelong learners and critical thinkers who are well prepared to navigate the information-rich society within the classroom and beyond. At Miami University, this approach is possible via the Faculty Learning Community (FLC) for Improving Student Research Fluency.

The Faculty Learning Community program at Miami University, housed within the Center for the Enhancement of Learning and Teaching (CELT), was established in 1978 and has offered more than eighty cohort-based or topic-based FLCs over the years (Richlin and Cox 2004). Each FLC may vary in goals and outcomes, but the underlying structure remains the same. The FLC environment fosters collaboration among a cross-disciplinary group of eight to twelve faculty and staff who engage in a yearlong program of discussions, seminars, retreats, and conferences with an emphasis on enhancing teaching and learning. The FLC for Improving Student Research Fluency was formed as a partnership between the University Libraries and CELT in 2004 to help foster the development of information fluency skills across the curriculum.

Developing a successful FLC model that promotes information literacy, while building upon liberal education and other curriculum-related principles, requires a multitiered approach. One crucial step is to develop a diverse group of participants who are invested in contributing to the community. FLC membership is determined through an application process wherein applicants share their personal desires and their interests in the topic. Once selected, community members participate over the course of an academic year in FLC retreats and seminars, explore readings on various topics, and take an in-depth look at courses to revise or create research-based assignments and integrate concepts discussed throughout the year. Having a commitment for an entire school year allows members to focus deeply on the topic, build relationships with one another, and experiment with infusing concepts within the classroom environment.

One of the hallmarks of a successful FLC is to provide a good balance of readings, projects, and discussions that engage all members. One activity that has been successful within the FLC for Improving Student Research Fluency is the "research exchange" conducted at the beginning of the year during the FLC retreat. Each community member is asked to write down a research topic of interest to them on an index card, and then members exchange topics with one another. Prior to the next meeting, each member is to find a couple of articles on the research topic. This activity provides members with an idea of what students experience when first conducting research in an unfamiliar area, and it creates an opportunity to collaborate with other community members.

In the three years since its inception, the FLC's members have represented seventeen different campus departments, and there have been numerous benefits and outcomes of the program, including improved course assignments, faculty obtaining a better understanding of resources available, and librarians developing a better understanding of assignment design and the information needs of specific courses. This FLC process has created faculty ambassadors who promote information literacy concepts within their departments and across campus, thus further enhancing the quality of student research campuswide.

Evolution of a Librarian: Instructional Designer Partnership in Higher Education

CONTRIBUTED BY KIM DUCKETT, DIGITAL TECHNOLOGIES AND LEARNING LIBRARIAN, AND DEDE NELSON, INSTRUCTIONAL DESIGNER, NORTH CAROLINA STATE UNIVERSITY

A partnership between a librarian and an instructional designer has helped faculty members in an online graduate program recognize the value of a collaborative model for course development and support. At North Carolina State University, Kim Duckett, a librarian specializing in digital technologies and learning, and Dede Nelson, an instructional designer in the Adult and Higher Education Department, began to recognize how the expertise from each of their professional roles could combine with a faculty member's content and teaching expertise to result in improved learning experiences for students. Kim and Dede have designed a model of the approach they use to collaborate with some of the faculty members in the courses they mutually support. They have also developed a "checklist" of library services that can easily inform faculty of ways to enhance their instructional efforts.

Since 2001 Kim had worked with the faculty and students in the university's first completely online master's degree program, Training and Development Online. In support of the interdisciplinary program, she developed a library portal of resources that the students could access through the learning management system in use for their program. She also routinely offered online library workshops using synchronous learning environments (i.e., Centra Symposium, Elluminate). Faculty members were pleased with this library support and encouraged students to attend workshops and contact Kim for library assistance. Nonetheless, despite these strong relationships, Kim was aware that the integration of library resources and instruction could be strengthened. Although Kim had access to all the online course environments through the learning management system, she felt as though she should only look at, but not touch, the course content. It was also difficult for her to achieve a systematic overview of the curriculum, assignments, and course learning objectives at the program level.

In August 2005 Dede began as instructional designer in the Adult and Higher Education Department with the role of supporting instructors teaching distance education courses. Initially she worked with faculty totally independently of Kim's efforts. Her relationship with the courses and faculty allowed her a broader view of faculty needs and instructional challenges from the program level. After reaching out to Kim about several library-related instructional needs, it became obvious that each had knowledge and available resources that could be mutually beneficial to the course development process. Dede discovered that Kim could provide invaluable information resources, copyright guidance, and knowledge about student cognitive gaps related to finding and evaluating information. On the other hand, Kim benefited from Dede's intimate knowledge of instructors' needs, plans for course and assignment modification, and general knowledge of instructional strategies and pedagogy.

Through their work, Kim and Dede have developed a collaborative model of course development and support in which instructors, instructional designers/instructional technologists, and librarians work together, often in an iterative cycle, to create an effective learning environment for students. Although not limited to specific functions in their roles, each partner has areas of expertise. The instructor provides a variety of skills and knowledge including content expertise, teaching experience, and an awareness of student pitfalls in the course. The instructor might also have instructional design and web design experience. The instructional designer works to ensure that targeted learning objectives are linked to specific learning activities and measurable outcomes. She also frequently assists the instructor with learning technologies and instructional strategies. The librarian provides expertise on course-appropriate resources, instructional support for students, information literacy objectives, copyright, and intellectual property. The flow of communication between these players takes many directions. Additionally, the student—as the center of the course development process—is a key player who can provide valuable feedback on the course through discussions, assignments or class activities, and assessments.

One example of this collaborative model at work was the development of a library-sponsored workshop called Introduction to Literature Reviews. After observing student difficulties with the overall research and writing process, Kim discussed her concern with Dede and several instructors, who were well aware of and concerned about the challenges students faced. Kim and a library colleague designed a workshop and offered it through a synchronous online classroom, using Elluminate Live. One instructor specifically required her students to attend the session, and the workshop was shaped to accommodate her assignments. This instructor provided feedback on the scope and content of the workshop, but all distance education students in the program were also encouraged to attend. Additionally, Dede leveraged the learning management system's tools to spread word of the workshop throughout several courses, as well as to promote the archived session to students after the event. Feedback from instructors and students was positive. Inspired by the idea of an instructor in the program, Kim and Dede have since begun to explore how the content could be redesigned as short modules that could be reused asynchronously throughout a variety of courses.

This example demonstrates how a librarian and instructional designer can join forces for mutual support of the teaching and learning needs of instructors and students. Additionally, Kim and Dede have also developed an online Library Services Checklist to share with other librarians, instructional designers, instructional technologists, and faculty. This tool, created as a series of questions and answers pertaining to instructional needs, is another example of how librarians and instructional designers can work together to support teaching and learning. It exposes a variety of library services, tools, and expertise of which many instructors and instructional support staff may not be aware. With this tool, Kim and Dede hope to encourage greater collaboration between librarians, instructional designers, and instructors at North Carolina State University.

By sharing their collaborative model of course development and the checklist, these partners have worked together to promote greater and better integration of library resources and instruction not only in the distance education courses in Adult and Higher Education but also across campus. Their collaboration illustrates the power of combining expertise, tools, and perspectives to enhance teaching and learning.

College Liaison Teams at St. Cloud State University

CONTRIBUTED BY CHRISTINE D. INKSTER, PROFESSOR, REFERENCE LIBRARIAN, AND ASSESSMENT COORDINATOR OF LEARNING RESOURCES AND TECHNOLOGY SERVICES; PLAMEN MILTENOFF, ASSOCIATE PROFESSOR, INSTRUCTIONAL DESIGNER, INFORMEDIA SERVICES; SANDRA Q. WILLIAMS, PROFESSOR, GOVERNMENT DOCUMENTS LIBRARIAN

Within the last decade, Learning Resources and Technology Services (LRTS) (http://lrts.stcloudstate.edu) at St. Cloud State University faced many changes and has evolved in adapting to them. The information technology and campus computing divisions became part of LRTS, the library established an "information commons" to integrate emerging technologies, and college technicians were hired to support faculty. Several years ago, LRTS opened a new facility, changed the campus e-mail program, adopted another course management software, and implemented a different integrated library system. In order to successfully initiate these new and evolving services, the improvement of our campus communications became a necessity. To address this critical need, we formed college liaison teams of librarians and other professionals from LRTS to serve as a communication vehicle for our myriad services.

The college liaison team program (http://lrts.stcloudstate.edu/instruction/liaisons/default.asp) has now operated for more than five years. Teams for each college include a reference librarian, another librarian, an instructional designer, and a technical specialist. Through the years we have encouraged college faculty to contact a college liaison team member for help with library and technology issues. The liaison, in turn, either finds the information or directs the faculty to the team member who can best help.

A variety of activities helped all liaisons understand the many services of LRTS. At retreats held early in the developmental process, LRTS work groups gave skits, presentations, or tours with accompanying handouts to highlight their campus services. The liaison team program is coordinated by a steering committee. Each college team meets regularly to plan college-specific activities and strives to meet annually with their college dean and department chairs, as well as with departments.

Since the program started, our liaison team for the College of Education (COE) has implemented a variety of activities, including helping with program accreditation, posting "timely tips" on the college's electronic discussion list, providing reference service to faculty and students in the COE's computer lab, orienting new faculty to library and technology services, selecting materials to support current and proposed curricula, and giving library instruction in LRTS classrooms as well as via interactive television and the course management system. Faculty have attended mini-sessions on such subjects as handheld devices, Minnesota e-Folio (a statewide electronic portfolio project), web development, course management software, digital image processing, blogging in classes, using clip art, and other library and technology topics. In addition, liaison team members make person-to-person "office calls" to help faculty with specific projects or problems regarding both the library and technology.

Challenges, of course, have come with implementing this new service. Over the years our teams have been faced with various problems. What services can be dropped if liaison activities become too time- or energy-consuming? How do we distinguish liaison work from regular professional responsibilities? What is the balance between service and servitude when working with other faculty? How can we encourage departments to find the time to meet with us? How can we evaluate the impact of liaison teams? Since some colleges have been more receptive to the liaison team concept than others, the success of the program has not been even across the university.

In the College of Education, results of the liaison team program have been positive. In spring 2005 our team surveyed the COE faculty and found that 86 percent of those responding were aware of the liaison team's services, with e-mail communications mentioned by 78 percent as the most important way they learned about us. Twenty-eight percent had attended a liaison-sponsored event, while 21 percent knew about the service from department meeting visits. More than half (57 percent) had contacted a liaison for both technical support and professional research assistance. Fifty-five percent had recommended that a colleague contact a liaison, 38 percent had shared information from a liaison with a colleague, and 28 percent had referred students to a liaison. More than a quarter of the COE faculty (28 percent) scheduled library instruction as a result of liaison efforts.

Our team's plans for the current academic year include an orientation for new faculty to be held in the Education Building rather than in the library; the continuation of e-mailed "timely tips" about new services and resources; mini-workshops on specific topics such as audience response systems; the extension of collection development for proposed doctoral programs; and collaborating with faculty to develop learning objects for library instruction in the online and distance learning environments.

Even though there continue to be challenges, we know that our campus communication has improved through the blending of skills involved in our liaison team collaborations. Throughout the process our personal technology, instructional design, and library skills have increased. Planning activities and then participating with our COE faculty colleagues has allowed each of us to extend our repertoire of technology, instruction, and library expertise. In turn, we are now able to provide effective and professional liaison assistance on a wider variety of topics and at greater depth to our COE faculty colleagues.

CONCLUSION

Collaboration with faculty, or other academic partners for that matter, is never easy to achieve. In our past blended librarian workshops we often hear that those who have established good collaborative relationships needed to make the first gesture. Whether it was adding a needed link to a courseware site, developing a resource page or tutorial for a unique assignment, or simply making a social connection in a cafeteria or campus cultural event, there are opportunities to create the connections that lead to better collaboration with faculty. But most of the anecdotal evidence we have gathered has a common core of discovering something that faculty value because it will save them time or create efficiencies. The WIIFM factor, while not the only path to collaboration with faculty, is in the blended librarian's view a method that succeeds a good deal of the time. But like many things that require a sacrifice of one's own time with no guarantee of success, there are risks. Efforts to create connections can and do fail. Where a connection was sought, none can be made. Like most investments, however, the rewards are certainly worth the risks taken if they result in a collaboration that enables academic librarians to support faculty's effort to help students achieve learning outcomes.

TOPICS FOR FURTHER DISCUSSION

To your way of thinking, what barriers do you see to collaboration with faculty? What barriers have you encountered at your institution?

Can you share an innovative collaboration program that you've heard or read about?

Do you collaborate with other academic support professionals on your campus, particularly those in the instructional design area? What projects or enhancements have come out of these collaborations?

Can you provide some examples of how you might use WIIFM to create a better connection with some of your faculty?

ADDITIONAL RESOURCE

Association of College and Research Libraries, Instruction Section, Teaching Methods Committee. 1997. "How to Build Librarian/Instructional Faculty Collaborative Partnerships." Poster session delivered at the annual conference of the American Library Association. http://www.ala.org/ala/acrlbucket/is/conferencesacrl/annual97/howbuildlibrarian.htm.

5 | Applying Blended Librarianship to Information Literacy through Course Management Systems

In order for technology to improve learning, it must "fit" into students' lives . . . not the other way around. —David Clark

OBJECTIVES

1. Identify the benefits of a course management system to the institution and its library.
2. Assess the differences of the system-level and course-level approaches of the A_FLIP model.
3. Explain the various methods librarians can use to integrate their resources and services into the course management system.

INTEGRATING THE LIBRARY INTO COURSEWARE

This chapter's primary focus is on the methods (i.e., the A_FLIP model) by which libraries can integrate themselves into course management systems (CMS) and learning management systems (LMS). CMS and LMS will primarily be referred to as "courseware" in our discussion of this topic. This integration is crucial because faculty and students are increasingly using courseware as a standard classroom tool. By incorporating library resources and services into courseware, the blended librarian will meet the students where they are. By offering a convenient and easy virtual point of service, the academic library is in a position to capitalize on the resource-sharing, communication, and assessment tools that courseware offers to enhance the library's instructional ability and its role both on and off campus.

This chapter builds on the previous chapters' discussion of the principles of design (i.e., the ADDIE and BLAAM models) and instructional technology. Course management systems, like any technology tool, can be misused. Too often technology is applied in an instructional process without design, and this leads to misuse. The wrong instructional tool for the wrong instructional process can be detrimental to and prevent the learner from learning. While reading this chapter and thinking about the various approaches that academic librarians can take to integrate with and utilize courseware, it is essential not to divorce the process of learner analysis, instructional design, development, and evaluation if one wants to achieve success.

A BRIEF CMS HISTORY, CURRENT STATUS, AND FUTURE TRENDS

The development and rise of the Internet has led to a plethora of new tools that facilitate communication and the sharing of information in digital formats. Courseware is one example of these newly emerging technologies that were developed in the late 1990s. These systems were initially created for the distance higher education market to allow students and instructors to form virtual classes that allowed greater communication, interaction, and resource sharing to occur. Shortly after the first generation of these systems was deployed, university and college administrators began to realize that there were benefits in using these systems to enhance traditional face-to-face classes. Faculty were encouraged to adopt these systems to help them more easily manage and communicate with their students.

Course management systems allow instructors to manage course support (i.e., share resources, communicate, and conduct assessment and record grades) and also deliver courses either partially or completely online. CMS are not the only types of systems that allow instructors to manage their courses; other systems that have similar functions are called learning management systems and learning content management systems (LCMS). While these systems are similar, LMS and LCMS are primarily used by industry in the United States, while outside the United States, LMS and LCMS are used by both industry and education. This chapter will focus solely on courseware (CMS/LMS) that is used in higher education in the United States.

Commercial and open source are the two primary types of CMS that are available in the United States. Currently, the commercial systems (i.e., Blackboard/WebCT, eCollege, ANGEL) account for over 80 percent of the systems used by the higher education market. Because of the expense and less customizable features of commercial CMS, open source CMS such as Moodle (Modular Object-Oriented Dynamic Learning Environment) and the Sakai Project (a joint venture started by Indiana University, Massachusetts Institute of Technology, University of Michigan, and Stanford University) are increasingly recognized as attractive alternatives to the commercial systems. It remains to be seen which commercial systems will continue to capture market share (for example, Blackboard and WebCT have agreed to merge) and whether open source begins to capture a larger percentage of the CMS market.

The use of courseware has dramatically increased over the past half decade. The vast majority of U.S. institutions of higher education have purchased a CMS. While the adoption rate by faculty has been at a slower pace, this too has considerably increased. The majority (two-thirds) of faculty who use CMS continue to make use of it for future courses (Morgan 2003). If the current adoption pace continues, a majority of U.S. college courses will make use of CMS before the end of this decade. Although CMS was initially designed for distance courses, it has increasingly come to be used to enhance traditional face-to-face classes (Cohen 2002). Warger (2003) asserts that "on most campuses, CMS products supplement traditional classroom courses." The speed at which CMS have been adopted at institutions of higher learning is nothing less than miraculous when you consider that these institutions have existed for centuries, have strong campus cultures and traditions, and tend to be skeptical of new technologies and, consequently, slow adopters.

Perhaps one reason behind the high adoption rate for course management systems is that they offer many tools that assist faculty in managing course documents, resources, and grades, as well as in communicating with and assessing their students. Many of the CMS offer similar features and tools (see Edutools, http://edutools.info). Most systems offer information management tools that allow faculty and students to share and edit files, create simple web pages, browse and link to external websites, display content such as PowerPoint, and organize the content within the instructor's course. These systems also provide a number of asynchronous (not at the same time) and synchronous (simultaneous) communication features. These include course e-mail, threaded message/discussion boards, and chat forums. Another key component of CMS are the assessment features. These include tools to import or create quizzes, to create surveys, and to provide feedback and assessment to the students' responses in quizzes or surveys, as well as grading management tools.

It is difficult to predict what tools future versions of CMS might have. There is little doubt that those systems will be faster, more flexible, easier to use, and have more functions that faculty and students desire. It is also likely that these systems will become even more integrated with other existing and developing web services that universities and colleges offer students, such as student portals, web storage space, e-mail, registrar, and file sharing. In this environment, students will expect to be able to perform more and more of these functions ubiquitously from the Web. Courseware is ideally positioned to be a primary system that students use to access enrollment, courses, university and nonuniversity resources, services, and communities. This makes it even more critical that the library integrate its staff, services, and resources into these systems.

CMS BENEFITS: RESOURCE SHARING, COMMUNICATION, ASSESSMENT

Currently, there are few studies and little research about the pedagogical benefits of using CMS. This is not surprising, since these systems have been used for less than a decade in higher education. Likewise, there is very little quantitative data about the impact and effects of using CMS to improve student learning. However, their rapid adoption and use by both faculty and students does provide some anecdotal evidence that these systems are seen as useful and beneficial by both groups. To better understand how libraries and librarians can make use of and more fully integrate their services into these systems, it is necessary to recognize what benefits these systems offer their users.

While there are a number of different courseware systems, the majority of these have a core set of standard functions and features that include resource sharing, communication tools, and assessment/evaluation tools. The resource-sharing features that most CMS offer are the ability to

- share files (including a syllabus)
- hypertext links
- provide a virtual classroom
- create simple web pages

The communication tools of most CMS include

- e-mail
- threaded message boards (asynchronous)
- electronic classroom, with a synchronous chat or message board
- synchronous chat room

The typical assessment tools offered by CMS are

- quiz creation and evaluation tools
- survey creation and evaluation tools
- student tracking tools

Resource Sharing

The resource-sharing capabilities of course management systems can be powerful tools that the instructor can use to enhance his or her instruction. CMS allow instructors and students to share an assortment of file types (e.g., word processing, spreadsheet, database, etc.) that can be accessed anytime and anywhere there is an Internet connection. This allows instructors to convert traditional paper-based handouts (e.g., syllabus, photocopied readings, exercises, assignments, etc.) to digital format and make them conveniently accessible to students outside the classroom. Furthermore, CMS allow instructors and students to link to web pages. This permits the instructor to create a library of resources (audiovisual materials, digital learning materials, monographs, and periodicals) as additional support materials for class lectures and texts.

Additionally, CMS allow users to easily create basic web pages. This enables faculty and students to create personalized web pages that can be used to enhance the course's existing resources (help/tip sheets and webquests). Finally, CMS have virtual whiteboards or classrooms that allow the class to meet synchronously online and share and edit files. The advantage of the resource-sharing capabilities of CMS is that they allow instructors to share and archive most if not all of their course content (texts, readings, assignments, tests) through creating, loading, or linking to documents and resources. Consequently, students find it easy and convenient to access their course information wherever and whenever they choose to.

Communication

Course management systems have an assortment of communication tools that allow instructors and students to communicate both synchronously and asynchronously independently of, and agreeable to, their locations and schedules. Most CMS have an internal e-mail tool that allows instructors and students to e-mail each other effortlessly (without needing to create class mailing lists). These e-mail systems also prevent spam and are more secure. Additionally, CMS have threaded message boards that allow students and instructors to communicate asynchronously. This enables faculty to continue or start new course discussions outside the classroom that can be archived and made available to students who need the information. This means that an instructor can provide a question-and-answer resource for a class that is continually updated and current.

Courseware also allows the class to meet through synchronous real-time chat forums that can be archived. Often, these chat clients are included in a virtual classroom. Currently, Voice over Internet Protocol (VoIP) is not a standard feature included in most courseware, but in the future this technology will allow the class to communicate synchronously and verbally. The considerable benefit of the communication features of a course management system is that they allow students to connect with their peers and instructor outside of the classroom and archive their discussions. Furthermore, they encourage class discussions by allowing shy students to have greater participation.

Assessment

The assessment and evaluation capabilities of course management systems allow the instructor and students to have greater feedback on student performance. CMS enable faculty to create quizzes and tests quickly and effortlessly. In addition, textbook publishers are increasingly making quizzes that can simply be imported and modified by the instructor. These quizzes then can provide immediate feedback on student responses both to the students who take them and the instructor, thereby allowing the instructor to identify students who are struggling to understand the course content.

Additionally, instructors can create surveys that can be used to provide student background information, student course evaluation, discussion topics, and much more. Furthermore, courseware allows instructors to monitor their students' use of course materials, as well as have access to grading management tools. The significant advantage of the assessment features of a CMS is that while the auto-marked and auto-feedback quizzes and surveys allow monitoring of student performance, they also reduce the grading time, thereby freeing up more of the instructors' time and allowing them to more efficiently focus on the areas where the students need the most assistance.

THE A_FLIP MODEL

The A_FLIP (Administrative, Faculty, and Librarians Instructional Partnership) model (Shank and Bell 2006) was created to demonstrate how to establish links between librarians, faculty, and courseware administrators in course management systems. As mentioned previously, the courseware environment is becoming an integral resource for both faculty and students to share course resources and communicate. Unfortunately, far too often the library and librarians are excluded from the CMS. (See figure 5-1.) This exclusion results in the library becoming increasingly marginalized and underutilized by both students and faculty. The A_FLIP model seeks to flip this dynamic so that students and faculty can quickly and easily move from their online course environment to the library and thereby further integrate the library into the classroom. Ultimately this allows the library to strengthen the information literacy environment across the curricula.

There are two approaches that can be used to integrate the library into the CMS. The system-level approach focuses on the types or techniques of integration that can be performed by collaborating with courseware programmers or administrators, while the course-level approach centers on cooperation between the librarians and faculty. Both of these approaches have strengths and weaknesses;

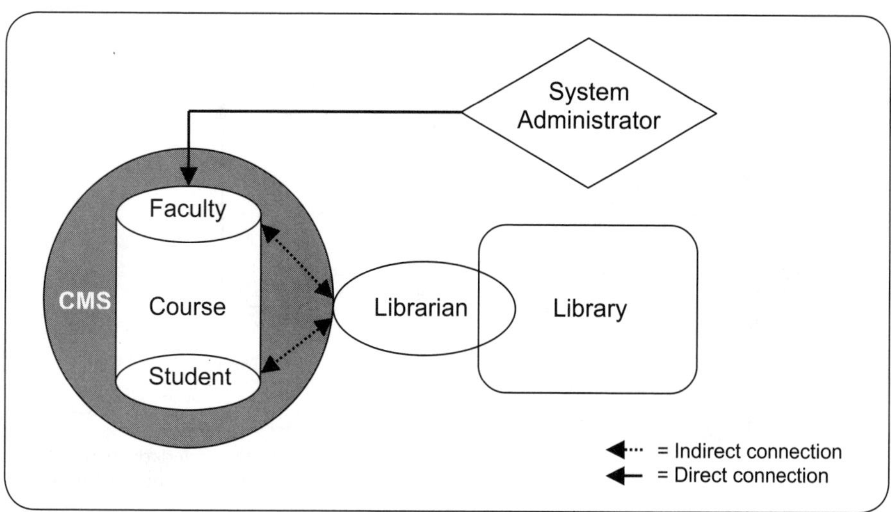

FIGURE 5-1
Traditional approach

therefore, each approach should be employed at the level that is most appropriate for the institutional circumstances.

The system-level approach (see figure 5-2) involves librarians collaborating with courseware administrators, developers, and programmers to integrate a standard, broad-based library presence in the courseware environment so that students can at the very least access the library's website and resources, thereby enabling students to easily and conveniently access a broad range of general library services and resources from within their course site. This approach takes advantage of the high level of scalability brought about by the integration of existing digital library services and resources with the management functions of courseware, permitting either large university or small college libraries to accomplish this integration effortlessly.

Minimally, the types of integration that could be made at the system level include the following.

1. Creating a global library presence in the CMS. This may entail creating an easily noticeable tab or button that links to the library's website or creating new and additional library courseware web pages appropriate for enhancing the students' access to library resources and services. The purpose behind establishing this link is to allow students to have simple and direct access to the library's online catalog and proprietary databases from the entire courseware.

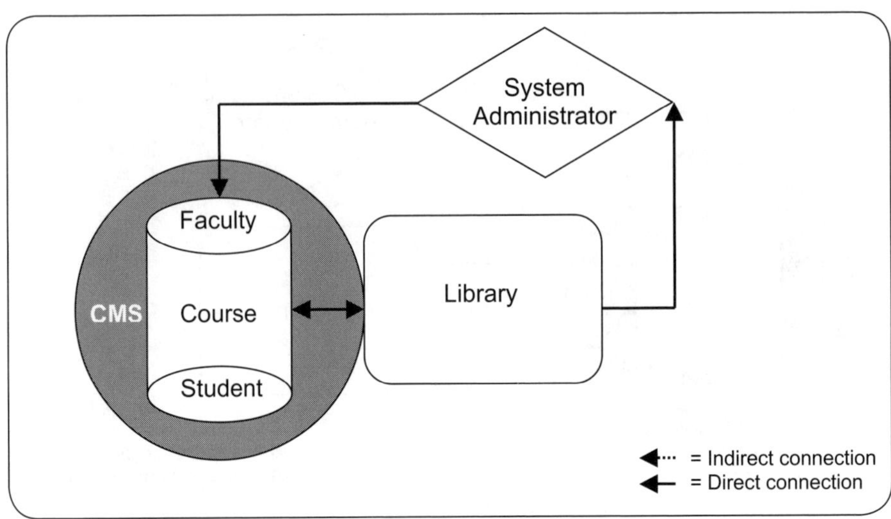

FIGURE 5-2
A_FLIP system-level approach

2. Creating a courseware tool that allows librarians to share pathfinders, bibliographies, and help sheets. This might involve creating preexisting templates that allow librarians to quickly and easily migrate existing pathfinders or create new ones. These templates would allow modification so that the pathfinders could be tailored for specific programs, curricula, or courses. Students would be able to use these pathfinders to access directly a list of relevant resources to assist them in completing their class assignments.
3. Creating or utilizing a preexisting location within a CMS course "splash" or log-in page that permits the library to post special announcements. This could entail taking advantage of a preexisting library blog or creating a courseware-specific blog and feeding it (through RSS) into the CMS. This would allow students to be informed of pertinent library resources and services directly from their course site.
4. Creating a user status for librarians that allows them (with an instructor's permission) to access, post resources, and communicate with students in their course sites. Additionally, it would be beneficial to allow library staff to create courses in order to become more familiar with the courseware tools and features. The student would be able to associate their course site with a specific librarian and communicate directly with them.

5. Creating or making use of preexisting virtual reference desk services in the CMS that would permit students to ask reference questions directly from their course site. Students would be able to have direct access to reference services regardless of their location and immediately on demand.
6. Creating or integrating an existing electronic reserves management system and other document delivery systems (i.e., interlibrary loan) that would enable faculty and students to post (digitize) and access readings electronically directly from their course sites.
7. Creating or utilizing existing web-based library tutorials and linking them to the courseware. These tutorials could introduce, enhance, and assess the students' information literacy knowledge and skills. Furthermore, these tutorials could be used to demonstrate how effectively the library is contributing to student learning outcomes for information literacy across the curricula.

There are a number of benefits that the system-level approach offers. By integrating the library into the courseware, students have an easy and convenient means by which to access the library's digital resources and services. This level of convenience encourages the students to use existing university-bought authoritative resources rather than just using free commercial search engines. Additionally, the library's presence in the courseware increases the library's visibility and reestablishes it as an essential place where students can locate and access course-related resources, thereby reemphasizing the library's relevance to the students. A third benefit, mentioned previously, is the high level of scalability that this approach offers. By integrating existing digital library services and resources within the courseware, libraries of any size can save staff time and resources. The only requirement is that small teams from the library work with the courseware staff to develop the technology to directly link the digital library services within the courseware. Finally, the system-level approach does not require faculty to commit any of their time to this integration process.

There are several disadvantages with using only the system-level approach. The greatest drawback is that it does not establish any direct face-to-face contact between the librarians and the students. This means that the students become more virtual/distance library users and may not feel comfortable using the library's physical resources and services. Additionally, the librarians may be less aware of potential gaps in student knowledge and skills (i.e., information literacy) and may not provide adequate services to address their needs in this environment. A secondary disadvantage is that this approach is not geared toward individual course customization. The systems approach seeks to maximize the library's broadest services and resources and does not seek to customize its resources and services to an individual or specific course.

In contrast to the system-level approach of the A_FLIP model, which focuses on collaboration at an institutional level, the course-level approach focuses on individual librarians and instructors working together in a partnership to offer more customized library research assistance within the students' course site (see figure 5-3). This approach is not meant to replace classroom library instruction sessions but rather to enhance or augment them. The course-level approach can be implemented at various levels of librarian participation. The least extensive would entail librarians providing faculty with digital resources in the form of documents or links to be imported by the instructor into the course, while the most extensive would allow the librarian to have equal access to the instructor's course, thereby enabling the librarian to add appropriate resources and monitor class communication (through e-mail, chat, or threaded message boards) for research-related questions.

Minimally, the types of integration that could be made at the course level include the following.

1. Creating a library instruction session outline that the students can access through the CMS prior to or after a librarian meets with the class to review a research assignment. This outline would augment the class session, providing relevant information so that students do not have to take extensive notes during the class session.

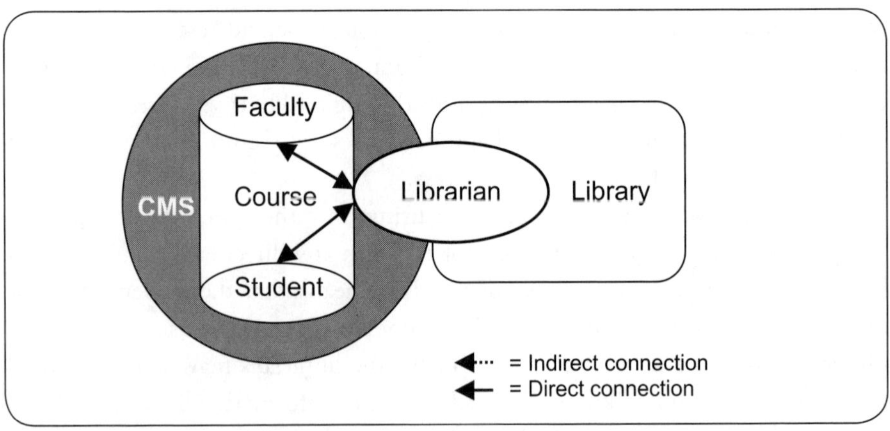

FIGURE 5-3
A_FLIP course-level approach

2. Creating customized pathfinders, bibliographies, and help sheets that are accessible to students in the courseware. These aids would be individualized for the instructor and course to assist students in completing their assignments. For example, students would be guided to appropriate databases and have access to a librarian's annotations or help sheets that explain how to effectively use and search the subject-appropriate library databases.
3. Creating assignment-specific APA, MLA, or other citation help sheets. These types of resources could help students with one of the most common reference questions by providing examples of their required citation format directly from their course site.
4. Creating links to suitable library sites and external websites that augment the course. These resources could include webliographies or appropriate subject matter sites.
5. Creating course-specific individualized reference services by having a librarian participate in course communication features such as e-mail, chat, or threaded message boards. At the very least, contact information should be provided so that students can call or e-mail a librarian. Ideally a librarian would be invited by an instructor to monitor course conversations (i.e., threaded message boards) in order to identify and answer library-appropriate research questions and, when possible, post these answers so that the entire class can see the question and answer.
6. Creating course-specific surveys to assess the preexisting skills of the students. This would help the librarian gain insight into the makeup of the class and the students' abilities. Students who might have more difficulty can be identified to receive additional support before they start their research assignments. Additionally, a follow-up questionnaire could be created to assist the librarian in evaluating the instruction session and the student-perceived quality of the session.
7. Creating course-specific pre- and post-test quizzes to assess the students' information literacy skills. These quizzes could be additional evidence in evaluating how effectively the library is contributing to student learning outcomes for information literacy.
8. Creating a librarian profile that allows the librarian to assist the instructor with assessing and observing the students' research assignment process through the "drop box" function, which allows students to submit their work electronically.

Like the system-level approach, the course-level approach has a number of strengths and some weaknesses. This model allows the librarian to establish a greater connection with the class than is possible by simply giving a one-shot library instruction session. One of the primary strengths of the course-level approach is that it allows librarians to customize resources for individual courses and tailor the resources for specific class assignments. This also benefits faculty members by saving them development and in-class time because it allows the librarian to provide customized resources for the instructor. Additionally, librarians benefit from developing a deeper cooperative relationship with faculty members, increasing their communications with the class. At the same time, librarians can strategically place library resources and services where they are needed the most and thereby avoid the pitfalls of having to direct students to the library's website, where they may have greater difficulty navigating and locating the information.

The benefit to the students is that this approach allows the librarian to respond directly to their specific needs where the assignments are posted, creating a context-specific, convenient one-stop shop for the students. The customized approach lends greater legitimacy and relevance to the library and librarian as being essential parts of the research process. This is an important difference between the system approach and the course approach in the A_FLIP model. The course approach is characterized by the customization of the content to that of an individual course instead of providing generic library resources to entire sections.

The greatest weakness of the course-level approach is that it may require librarians to invest significantly more time in developing resources and supporting the research assignments of each course. This effect could multiply if librarians have a great deal of success because multiple faculty, who teach dozens of courses and have hundreds of students, may seek out librarians to implement this approach and thereby possibly create challenges for many libraries because of staffing limitations. However, the course-level approach is only now emerging as a standard practice, and there is very little research to indicate what might be appropriate librarian-to-instructor course ratios. This leaves it up to each institution to use its best judgment in determining acceptable ratios. Librarians becoming more integrated into courseware at the course level could lead to greater efficiencies being achieved in collaborating with faculty through the courseware environment.

In addition, this model can only be as successful as the level at which faculty are willing to give librarians permission to access their courses and develop faculty-librarian partnerships. This means that it is vital to work initially with those faculty who feel strongly that this model will benefit them and their class and thereby showcase the successes that librarians have working with these faculty to the rest of the institution. Moreover, developing these faculty as faculty-librarian partnership champions may help other faculty buy into the approach.

CONCLUSION

Course/learning management systems are still relatively new to faculty and students, and these systems will continue to evolve and mature. It is vital to the library and librarians to make use of and establish services in these systems so that students and faculty alike recognize the value that the library brings to this environment. Additionally, the library will be less likely to be bypassed or marginalized by students if they have an easy and convenient means to access the resources they need through their courseware. Librarians need to capitalize on the pedagogical and course management benefits that these systems offer in order to strengthen their connections with faculty, increase course integration, and enhance their instruction.

The A_FLIP model provides a framework that can facilitate the integration of the library and its services into the courseware environment. There is no "one size fits all" approach to this integration. Librarians need to design their own instructional programs for using the various methods in the system-level approach or the course-level approach. It is important to utilize both approaches to some degree, because each of these models has different advantages and disadvantages. If these approaches are designed and implemented effectively, the library will once again be the center for research and learning that it has been in the past. The only difference is that instead of being at the center of the university or college in only a physical sense, it will also be the center in a virtual sense.

CASE STUDY

The following case study examines how Nancy Dewald, a reference librarian at the Berks campus of Penn State University, partnered with a faculty member who teaches business courses to provide access to library resources at the course level for the instructor's research assignment. This case study is an example of how a librarian-faculty partnership through courseware can enable the librarian to augment class instruction and provide useful resources in an easy and convenient location for students to access.

A Librarian-Faculty Partnership at Penn State University, Berks Campus

I began to provide course-related instruction for a senior-level business course titled Contemporary Business Seminar several years ago. This course requires a large research and writing assignment that includes doing an industry analysis or company analysis. Because there were many business databases to demonstrate to the class, I developed some exercises for the students to do. I also pointed them to the short Flash database help tutorials on the website of the Business Library at Penn State's University Park campus for future reference. However, these were not easy for the students to locate and may not have gotten much use.

Then the professor decided to make the course available in ANGEL, Penn State University's course management system. I requested and received permission from her to add library resources. This involved her adding me to the ANGEL course as "Librarian" with editing privileges. I sent her instructions on how to do this.

ANGEL allows a librarian as editor to add links to databases and websites, add explanations and tips for using these resources, upload Word documents, import multimedia (such as Flash movies), and organize the resources in folders. The best advantage of all is the strategic placement of the Library Resources folder next to the professor's assignment. Students regularly go into ANGEL for the many resources placed there by the professor, and situating the Library Resources folder near the course assignment makes it easy and convenient for students to access the library resources.

I present the folder when I go to their class, explaining its organization and use and giving them an exercise to begin using a few of the databases. They have access to the folder throughout the entire semester, and the in-class practice will remind them of its usefulness later. Once the folder is created, I can import it into future sections of the course, saving my time in succeeding semesters.

This Library Resources folder includes the following (see figure 5-4):

- Several database folders, each of which contains
    - A link to a business database. The links are obtained from the university libraries' website and ensure that authenticated users have direct access to the database.
    - Brief tips for using the database for this particular assignment.
    - Links to very short Flash help tutorials that demonstrate the basics of using that database. These tutorials were created by the Business Library, and I obtained permission to link to them.
- A folder of links to U.S. government websites appropriate for business research.
- A page of tips for searching some of the specific items mentioned in the assignment, such as SWOT analysis (strengths, weaknesses, opportunities, threats), finding market share, researching "power of suppliers" and "power of customers," and locating trade associations.

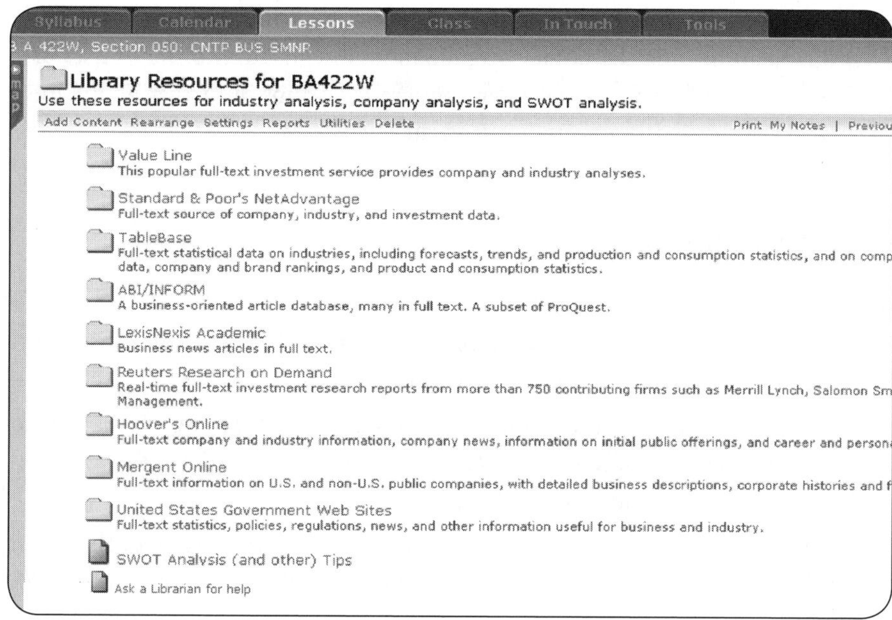

FIGURE 5-4
Library Resources folder in the business ANGEL website

- My APA style handout.
- My contact information.

This customized folder grew out of my long-standing partnership with the professor for this course. It is customized to this assignment, and it enhances my presentation to the class while remaining available to the students throughout the semester. Students have the opportunity to try out the databases with a particular exercise in the library class, and the Flash help tutorials are available as needed later in the semester to provide a refresher for students who might have forgotten how to use them effectively.

TOPICS FOR FURTHER DISCUSSION

How is your library integrating its services into the CMS at your institution?

What are the comparative advantages and disadvantages of using the system-level and the course-level approaches of the A_FLIP model to integrate your library's services into the CMS?

How many of your library's resources and services could be integrated into your institution's CMS?

Can you identify a faculty member, or more than one, who would be particularly valuable in helping the library become more integrated into the courseware? If so, how might you capitalize on these relationships in furthering the integration of the library into the courseware?

ADDITIONAL RESOURCES

Bell, Steven J., and John D. Shank. "Academic Libraries and Course Management Software: A Resource Page for Librarians, Instructional Technologists, Systems Administrators." http://staff.philau.edu/bells/cmsresourcepage.htm.

———. 2004. "Linking the Library to Courseware: A Strategic Alliance to Improve Learning Outcomes." *Library Issues: Briefings for Faculty and Administrators* 25, no. 2 (November): 1–4.

Bhavnagri, Navaz P., and Veronica Bielat. 2005. "Faculty-Librarian Collaboration to Teach Research Skills: Electronic Symbiosis." *Reference Librarian* 89/90: 121–38.

Bongiorno, Rachel, Patricia G. Hinegardner, Virginia L. Stone, and Mary Ann Williams. 2004. "Delivery of Web-Based Instruction Using Blackboard: A Collaborative Project." *Journal of the Medical Library Association* 92, no. 3 (July): 375–77.

Buehler, Marianne A. 2004. "Where Is the Library in Course Management Software?" *Journal of Library Administration* 41, nos. 1/2: 75–84.

Costello, Barbara, Robert Lenholt, and Judson Stryker. 2003. "Utilizing Blackboard to Provide Library Instruction: Uploading MS Word Handouts with Links to Course Specific Resources." *Reference Services Review* 31, no. 3: 211–18.

———. 2004. "Using Blackboard in Library Instruction: Addressing the Learning Styles of Generations X and Y." *Journal of Academic Librarianship* 30, no. 6 (November): 452–60.

Cox, C. 2002. "Becoming Part of the Course." *College and Research Libraries News* 63, no. 1 (January): 11–13.

Cubbage, Charlotte. 2003. "Electronic Reserves and Blackboard's Course Management System." *Journal of Interlibrary Loan, Document Delivery and Information Supply* 13, no. 4: 21–32.

George, Julie, and Kari Martin. 2004. "Forging the Library Courseware Link: Providing Library Support to Students in an Online Classroom Environment." *College and Research Libraries News* 65, no. 10 (November): 594–97, 613.

Getty, N. K., B. Burd, S. K. Burns, and L. Piele. 2000. "Using Courseware to Deliver Library Instruction via the Web: Four Examples." *Reference Services Review* 28, no. 4: 349–59.

Jones, Jaclyn, Cait Kokolus, and Lisa McColl. 2004. "Tailoring Oversize Courseware to Fit Our Small Library." *Computers in Libraries* 24, no. 8 (September): 16–18, 20, 22.

Kraemer, Elizabeth W. 2003. "Developing the Online Learning Environment: The Pros and Cons of Using WebCT for Library Instruction." *Information Technology and Libraries* 22, no. 2 (June): 87–92.

Long, Phillip D. 2002. "Can Libraries Find a New Home in Courseware?" *Syllabus* 15 (March). http://www.syllabus.com/article.asp?id=6136.

Lovett, Deborah G. 2004. "Library Involvement in the Implementation of a Course Management System." *Medical Reference Services Quarterly* 23, no. 1 (Spring): 1–11.

Martin, K. B., and J. Lee. 2003. "Using a WebCT to Develop a Research Skills Module." *Issues in Science and Technology Librarianship* 37 (Spring). http://www.istl.org/03-spring/article5.html.

McColl, Lisa, Jaclyn Jones, and Cait Kokolus. 2005. "E-Courses: Tailoring Courseware to Fit Our Small Library." *Catholic Library World* 76, no. 1 (September): 22–26.

Shank, J. D., and N. H. Dewald. 2003. "Establishing Our Presence in Courseware: Adding Library Services to the Virtual Classroom." *Information Technology and Libraries* 22, no. 1 (March): 38–43. http://www.lita.org/ala/lita/litapublications/ital/vol22no1march.htm.

Yi, Hua. 2005. "Library Instruction Goes Online: An Inevitable Trend." *Library Review* 54, no. 1: 47–58.

6 Low Threshold Applications
Helping Faculty Focus on New Technology

New technologies can dramatically improve time on task for students and faculty members. —Arthur Chickering and Steve Ehrmann

OBJECTIVES

1. Explore the challenges of connecting faculty with library technologies.
2. Learn what low threshold applications are and how they can help meet these challenges.
3. Discover the process for developing a low threshold application.

LESS TIME ON TECHNOLOGY AND MORE ON LEARNING

In chapter 4 we discussed the value of collaboration with faculty and presented ideas for promoting greater collaboration with them at your institution. One of the ways in which academic librarians can achieve collaboration with faculty is by introducing them to new technology, and not just any instructional technology, but library technology. In chapter 4 we also mentioned some of the key factors that contribute to laying the groundwork for greater collaboration. One of those was the WIIFM ("What's in it for me?") factor. A faculty member can be encouraged to learn how to make use of a new library technology if he or she believes there is something in it for his or her own professional development, or if you can reduce the amount of time it takes him or her to learn a new technology that can provide benefits to both teacher and students.

The seven key principles for promoting good teaching and learning point to the importance of getting students to spend more time on learning tasks. Faculty can use library technology to engage students in research by getting them to spend more time on research assignments. But for faculty, blended librarians can help them use technology to spend *less* time on mundane tasks and also make it possible to learn about library technologies in less time. This means faculty can spend more time on their critical tasks: teaching and research. Getting faculty to sit down and learn any new technology is difficult at the best of times. Quite simply, faculty are typically reluctant to invest significant time learning new technologies. This is where low threshold applications (LTAs) can play a role in advancing the collaboration mission of the academic librarian while engaging faculty in learning how to use new library technologies.

The term *low threshold application* refers to a technology or technology application that offers a low threshold; that is, it can be mastered without great difficulty if presented in a way that makes it quick and relatively easy to learn. Though LTAs can be used by anyone to learn new technologies, their original intent was to enable faculty at higher education institutions to painlessly learn how to adapt an instructional technology for teaching and learning applications. LTAs are practical in nature and evolved as a response to faculty who claimed that learning new instructional technologies and integrating them into their courses was time-consuming and overwhelming.

The LTA was an initiative started by the Teaching, Learning, and Technology Group as a way to share and promote good ideas developed by instructional technologists and faculty for integrating technology into the classroom. The TLT Group, founded in 1996, is an organization that includes as members more than 900 educational institutions, associations, and corporations around the world. A primary objective of the TLT Group is to improve teaching and learning by making more appropriate and cost-effective use of information technology. The TLT Group's biggest asset is its network of hundreds of leaders and institutions working together to solve common problems and share effective strategies. That, in part, is how LTAs are developed and made available on the Internet. They represent a cooperative effort by the members of the TLT Group. More information about the TLT Group is found at their website, at http://www.tltgroup.org.

LTAs are still in the process of becoming more widely known to the academic library community. This chapter will provide background information on the development of LTAs, explain what they are and how they are created, examine ways in which they can be used to both promote the use of library technologies and enhance collaboration between faculty and librarians, and present a case study in the development of an LTA. There is almost no limit to the types of library technology applications that could make good LTAs. All it takes to make them happen are good ideas and some relatively easy design and development work.

PROMOTING THE ACADEMIC LIBRARY AS CAMPUS TECHNOLOGY LEADER

In 2002 the Association of College and Research Libraries published a report titled "Top Issues Facing Academic Libraries: A Report of the Focus on the Future Task Force" (Hisle 2002). This article on the top challenges facing academic librarians at that time identified seven critical issues. A central theme running through the report is that librarians "must demonstrate to the campus community that the library remains central to academic effort" (Albanese 2003). This issue, though identified several years ago, remains just as essential to the success of academic libraries today. One important way that these libraries can continuously work to remain at the core of the academic enterprise is to establish a role as campus technology leaders. Some academic librarians may ask how that is possible when the majority of institutional technology may be under the control of the information technology department or an educational or academic technology unit. The academic library is not without its own technologies, however, and as blended librarians we need to play a role in using those technologies to establish the library's ability to contribute to technology integration.

What better way to do that than by collaborating with faculty to further integrate library technologies and resources into the teaching and learning process? The challenge is how to influence and encourage faculty to open up the curriculum and classroom to librarians. Overcoming that challenge offers blended librarians an excellent opportunity to apply design thinking in identifying solutions and creating instructional products that will promote the use of library technologies and the librarian's role as campus technology leader. A good example is provided by LTA no. 36, which explains how faculty can use RSS and news aggregators to save time spent keeping up with news and information sources, and potentially use the technology to help keep students alert to important news relevant to course topics. At the time this LTA was developed, in 2004, RSS technology was relatively new and not much used by faculty. But this LTA was developed by an academic librarian, not an information or instructional technologist. Academic librarians often play the role of "early adopter" on their campuses, and this was an opportunity to design an instructional product that would encourage and enable faculty to adopt this new technology in a step-by-step instructional approach. Blended librarians can proactively promote the adoption of new technologies, and in doing so they develop a reputation among faculty for technology leadership.

USING TEACHNOLOGIES TO BREAK DOWN BARRIERS TO FACULTY INTEGRATION OF TECHNOLOGY

Faculty resistance to learning library technologies is more complex than lack of awareness or gross underestimation of what librarians can offer. Rather, faculty members are often too busy with teaching or research responsibilities to find the time to learn how to make the best use of library resources. Some library technologies, though familiar to librarians, may seem daunting to faculty. Bibliographic or full-text database search systems represent a significant learning challenge for faculty. Aside from the multiplicity of these systems, their syntax features differ widely, and mastering any of them is a challenging task. The goal of an LTA is to make any type of educational technology easy and convenient for faculty to learn and use. If they have not done so already, academic librarians must shift away from their traditional perception of electronic library resources as search-and-retrieval systems and instead recognize and promote them to faculty as educational and instructional technologies. It may help us to think of our array of computer-based information resources as "teachnologies" owing to their ability to blend teaching and technology to enhance student learning (Bell 2004).

Like the authors, many individuals learned about the LTA concept from Steve Gilbert, the president of the TLT Group. If your institution has a TLT Group–affiliated Teaching, Learning, and Technology Roundtable, you are probably familiar with Gilbert and his innovative thinking about technology's impact on higher education. Or you may be among those librarians who have encountered him at one of his many appearances at academic librarian and higher education conferences. As Gilbert has described it in the past, the rationale for developing LTAs was to help overcome the barriers that faculty encounter when attempting to integrate technology into their teaching and student learning. Common barriers include inadequate time to learn and implement the technologies, perceptions that they are too complicated and confusing, and the lack of release time or resources.

What technology innovations would faculty most likely resist? Gilbert has observed that faculty will avoid almost any technology that takes more than thirty minutes to learn, requires more than a page of documentation, or carries any associated budgetary costs. The LTA concept is Gilbert's solution to the technology aversion problem. LTAs are economical, easy to learn, and conveniently available technologies that faculty can integrate into their face-to-face or web-based courses. While the TLT Group provides a website that collects and promotes

LTA ideas submitted by group members, faculty are still challenged to find LTAs that are locally available. The library can be a source of unique and abundant low threshold applications, all of which are easy to learn and available at no cost to faculty.

WHAT IS AN LTA?

This chapter has already provided some clues about what an LTA is. Perhaps the easiest way to describe it is that an LTA uses simple step-by-step instructions in providing a hands-on method to learn a new technology. A more formal definition can be found on the TLT website:

> A Low Threshold Application (LTA) is a teaching/learning application of information technology that is reliable, accessible, easy to learn, non-intimidating and (incrementally) inexpensive. Each LTA has observable positive consequences, and contributes to important long term changes in teaching and/or learning . . . The potential user (teacher or learner) perceives an LTA as NOT challenging, not intimidating, not requiring a lot of additional work or new thinking. LTAs are also "low-threshold" in the sense of having low incremental costs for purchase, training, support, and maintenance. (http://www.tltgroup.org/resources/ltas.html)

In a presentation about LTAs conducted at one of the authors' campuses several years ago, Steve Gilbert identified the key characteristics of an LTA. An LTA is a combination of technical and pedagogical components and has the following characteristics:

It enhances productivity without intimidating, does not require major adjustments in a faculty member's life, and should easily fit into existing teaching and learning methods.

It provides observable positive outcomes; improvements as a result of the LTA should be confirmed through anecdotal results from faculty and students.

It is easy to learn, is based on applications that are reasonably well known, and ideally takes as little as thirty minutes and no more than sixty minutes to learn.

It is easy to access, is available to all interested parties at their institution, and requires no special privileges to obtain.

It requires minimal documentation; nothing more than a sheet, if anything is needed beyond what appears on the LTA resource page.

It is known for reliability; should be available when it is needed, especially in the classroom; and does not require support from an academic or technology support team.

It precipitates or facilitates long-term change; use of the technology has the potential to create change in the teaching and learning process.

It is available at a low incremental cost; does not require significant hardware, software, or infrastructure additions; and is based on a technology that is almost ubiquitous and essential for academic institutions.

As you read these characteristics, did the phrase "sounds like a library technology" come to mind more than once? Let's examine this more closely.

It enhances productivity—why spend hours trying to hunt down quality information on websites when you can find it on the right library database in a tenth of the time?

It provides observable outcomes—rare is the faculty member who won't be pleased to see students using quality information sources instead of nothing but websites.

It is easy to learn—most library databases have a minimal learning curve because they offer multiple search interfaces for beginners as well as experts; advanced features take longer to learn. Once the basics are learned, that knowledge can be quickly transferred to additional library databases.

It is easy to access—most colleges and universities make their library databases accessible to all faculty and students from anywhere they have connectivity.

It requires minimal documentation—while the library's electronic resources present a slight learning curve, in most cases they can be used without the need for written or online documentation.

It is known for reliability—although this can certainly be affected by the quality of the institutional network and the occasional technical glitch, in general the library's electronic resources are available and ready to use 24/7 with rare downtime.

It precipitates long-term change—the library's electronic resources can have a tremendous impact on how individuals find and use high-quality information; they can create behavioral change in how individuals approach and conduct the process of information retrieval.

It is available at a low cost—since the library has already acquired the appropriate resources, there is never any cost to faculty.

To promote the development and sharing of LTAs, the TLT Group sponsors an LTA section on its website. The LTA home page is found at http://www.tltgroup.org/ltas.htm, and the inventory of existing LTAs is found at http://zircon.mcli.dist.maricopa.edu/lta/. (See figures 6-1 and 6-2.) An LTA is really a simply designed and formatted tutorial. Most are a set of textual step-by-step instructions

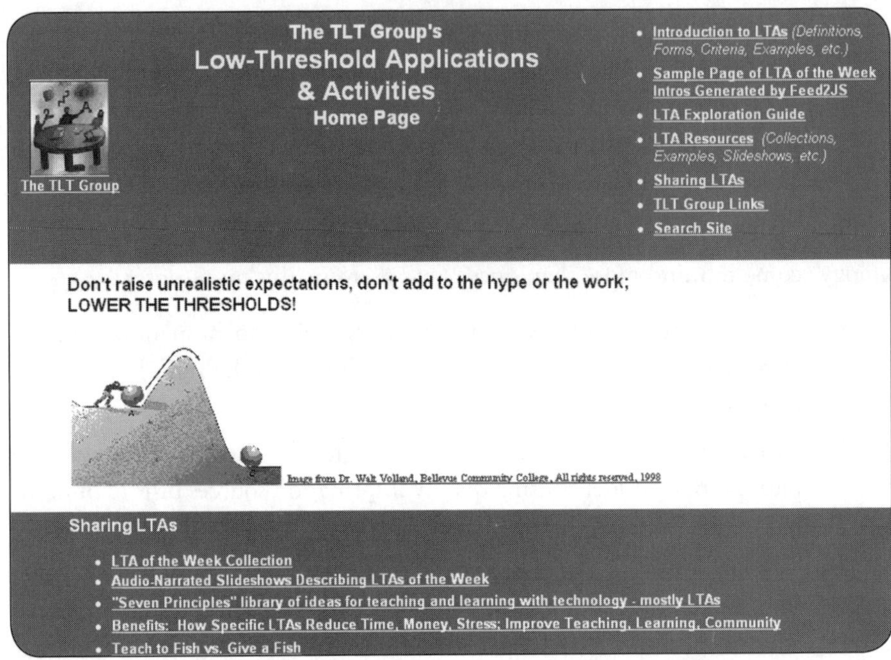

FIGURE 6-1

Low Threshold Applications home page

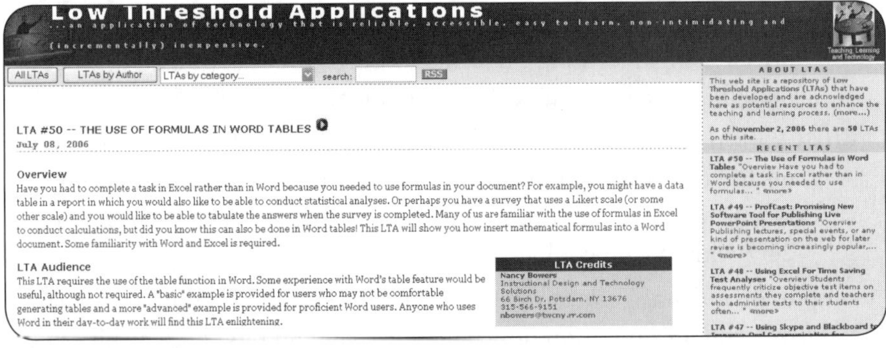

FIGURE 6-2

LTA example no. 50: Use of formulas in Word tables

supplemented with screen shots or links. Creating an LTA requires little more than a word processor and screen-capture software, although some may incorporate or link to a supplemental digital learning object. All LTAs are edited to ensure consistency and ease of use. Examples of the technology applications described in LTAs include "Integrating RSS Feeds into Courseware Sites," "Using Digitized

Recordings to Respond to Student Writing," and "Partnering with Students to Avoid Cut and Paste Plagiarism." All of these LTAs are designed to introduce faculty to a new technology application that can help save time spent on mundane tasks, enhance communication with students, or promote any of the other seven principles for good implementation of technology and do so in a minimal amount of time with little learning curve.

LTAS FOR ACADEMIC LIBRARIES AND THEIR USERS

Most library technologies are typically perceived by both librarians and faculty as information gateways. That is, the library's electronic resources are ways to get to the journal articles, books, and other content that faculty and students need to use for their research. In our ongoing effort to better integrate the library into the teaching and learning process, blended librarians need to do a better job of promoting the library's electronic resources as instructional technologies. The goal is to have faculty identify these resources as tools that can be enlisted to help their students achieve learning outcomes, in the same way they might think of a video presentation, a PowerPoint slide show, a webcast of a subject expert, or some other digital learning material. This might be the most powerful application of an LTA for a library resource because it not only helps the faculty member or student to learn to use the resource, but it can also demonstrate how that resource can be effectively applied in a teaching and learning environment.

We know that library resources make good LTAs. There is no added cost to the user community for these resources; the library has already paid for them. When LTAs encourage greater use of the academic library's electronic content, that is beneficial to the entire community. While library resources have sometimes been criticized for being too complex, they are hardly beyond the learning capacity of any member of our academic community. Despite a modest learning curve, when aided by an LTA, faculty members can learn how to use these resources for specific teaching and learning applications in less than an hour—and they certainly offer the WIIFM factor, because in the long run the learning time invested will reap many hours of saved instructional and research time. Library technologies ultimately increase faculty productivity by creating easier-to-navigate paths to needed content for teaching and research.

As technology revolutionizes and permeates education, there are concerns that the library will be increasingly marginalized. The challenge, as presented in the ACRL's Focus on the Future report, is for academic librarians to find ways to further integrate the library into the teaching and learning process. How can we do this? Let's consider courseware management systems as an example. LTAs, when developed for use with widely used courseware, can make a difference by giving faculty an easy and convenient mechanism for creating linkages between their course site and the library's information resources. Consider the durably linked database article. At many academic institutions, faculty members continue to provide classroom readings of these for students by scanning hard-copy articles, reformatting them in graphics software, and then uploading them to their course sites; it's also likely that many more faculty continue to simply photocopy articles and distribute them in class.

Many of these faculty readings, particularly the ones that come from newspapers, magazines, and trade publications, are increasingly available as full-text articles in library databases. Imagine how much easier and time-saving it is for faculty to simply locate the article in a library database and then incorporate a link to that article from within their courseware site. It is then quite easy to alert students to the existence of the link by e-mail, and because the link allows students to quickly access the article and read it in advance of a class discussion, it is a pedagogically advantageous method to improve classroom discussions. A durable link is a URL that is unique to an article in a library database (such links are growing more common, although they might not yet be found in every library database), and the URL persists over time. If a faculty member uses that link within their courseware site, it can be used over and over again each semester, since the link will continue to point to that article for as long as the library maintains its database subscription. Figure 6-3 illustrates links to library database articles within the courseware site, and figure 6-4 illustrates how the full article (from the ProQuest database system) appears in the courseware site after students click the link.

As they discover that many of their course readings are available as electronic content through the library, faculty will increasingly be able to simply create "e-reserves" within their course sites. This can be a tremendous time-saver for faculty because the durable links will persist and can be used each semester without the instructor having to rebuild the e-reserve component of the course. In order to facilitate the faculty's ability to make use of these persistent links within library databases, LTA no. 26, "Durable Links and Downloads: Create E-Reserves with Library Content" (found at http://zircon.mcli.dist.maricopa.edu/lta/archives/lta26.php), was created by an academic librarian (see figure 6-5). This was the first of several library technology-based LTAs created to both promote library technologies as learning resources and make them easier for faculty to integrate into their courses. What are some of the other existing and potential LTAs for library technologies?

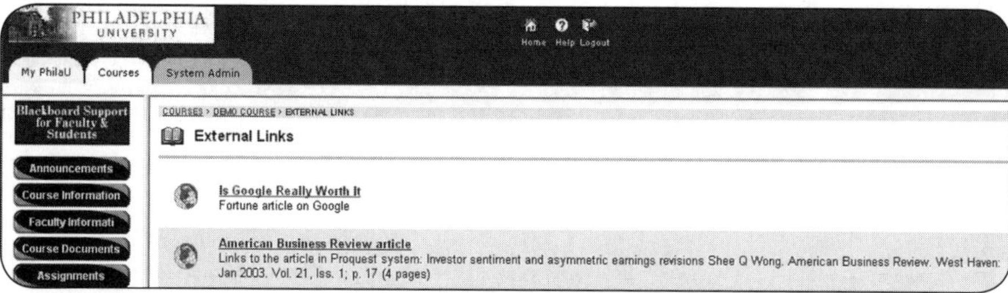

FIGURE 6-3
Library content integrated into a Blackboard course site

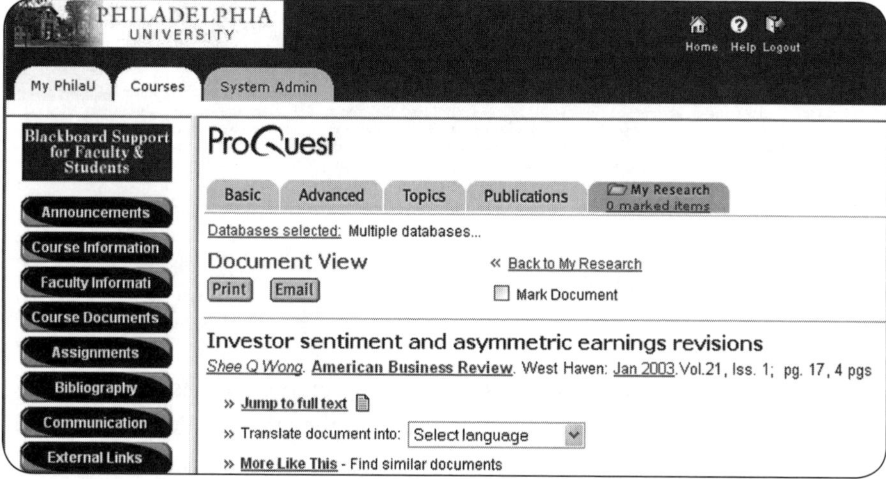

FIGURE 6-4
Viewing an article in a Blackboard course site

IDENTIFYING AND DEVELOPING LTAS

The challenge comes in identifying library-based LTAs that will appeal to faculty. But given their abundant technology resources, libraries can serve as a plentiful source of LTAs. LTA novices should begin their journey at the TLT Group's LTA website. The site is actually maintained by Charles A. Ansorge, faculty development leader at the Teaching and Learning Center at the University of Nebraska at Lincoln. The LTA site, at http://zircon.mcli.dist.maricopa.edu/lta/, features the "Current LTA" as well as the archive of all past LTAs, which contains over fifty examples. The TLT Group actively promotes the development and sharing of LTAs by its member network. Anyone is free to contribute a new LTA, and librarians are encouraged to add to the growing archive. Since we have many technologies

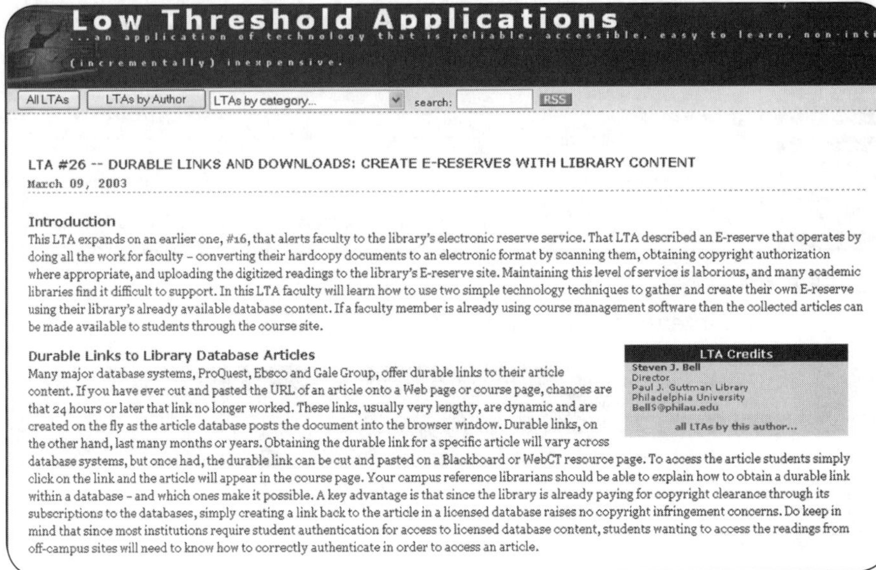

Low Threshold Applications

...an application of technology that is reliable, accessible, easy to learn, non-intin

(incrementally) inexpensive.

All LTAs | LTAs by Author | LTAs by category... | search: | RSS

LTA #26 -- DURABLE LINKS AND DOWNLOADS: CREATE E-RESERVES WITH LIBRARY CONTENT

March 09, 2003

Introduction

This LTA expands on an earlier one, #16, that alerts faculty to the library's electronic reserve service. That LTA described an E-reserve that operates by doing all the work for faculty – converting their hardcopy documents to an electronic format by scanning them, obtaining copyright authorization where appropriate, and uploading the digitized readings to the library's E-reserve site. Maintaining this level of service is laborious, and many academic libraries find it difficult to support. In this LTA faculty will learn how to use two simple technology techniques to gather and create their own E-reserve using their library's already available database content. If a faculty member is already using course management software then the collected articles can be made available to students through the course site.

Durable Links to Library Database Articles

Many major database systems, ProQuest, Ebsco and Gale Group, offer durable links to their article content. If you have ever cut and pasted the URL of an article onto a Web page or course page, chances are that 24 hours or later that link no longer worked. These links, usually very lengthy, are dynamic and are created on the fly as the article database posts the document into the browser window. Durable links, on the other hand, last many months or years. Obtaining the durable link for a specific article will vary across database systems, but once had, the durable link can be cut and pasted on a Blackboard or WebCT resource page. To access the article students simply click on the link and the article will appear in the course page. Your campus reference librarians should be able to explain how to obtain a durable link within a database - and which ones make it possible. A key advantage is that since the library is already paying for copyright clearance through its subscriptions to the databases, simply creating a link back to the article in a licensed database raises no copyright infringement concerns. Do keep in mind that since most institutions require student authentication for access to licensed database content, students wanting to access the readings from off-campus sites will need to know how to correctly authenticate in order to access an article.

LTA Credits

Steven J. Bell
Director
Paul J. Guttman Library
Philadelphia University
BellS@philau.edu

all LTAs by this author...

FIGURE 6-5

LTA example no. 26: Durable links

in common, why not share our ideas on how to promote their use to faculty? To date, there are only a few library-specific LTAs in the archive. A review of previously accepted LTAs provides good examples of the technologies that make good LTAs. All of the currently available library-related LTAs are found at http://zircon.mcli.dist.maricopa.edu/lta/archives/cat_librarybased_resources.php.

Gilbert's criteria for or characteristics of LTAs must be carefully kept in mind when conceiving a library-based LTA. Our technologies are free to faculty, so they must meet the "highly economical" test. Next, think about technologies that require thirty minutes or less for an individual to walk themselves through the steps to completion. Finally, if supporting documentation is produced, can it fit on a single page? In fact, most LTAs are web-based, consolidating all the instructions on a single page, and often no additional documentation is needed. Gilbert points out that an LTA can also identify a technology that saves faculty time or enhances productivity. The greatest inspiration for potential LTAs will come from faculty. Academic librarians can identify LTA topics by paying attention to where faculty are experiencing frustration with library technologies or are merely unaware of them. Potential library LTAs include

- Using the library's catalog-based or turnkey system e-reserve (already an existing LTA)

- Creating personal search alerts in databases and e-journal collections
- Locating articles in databases using exact citations, supplementing the addition of specific articles to course sites or e-reserves
- Exporting citations from a library database into personal bibliographic software
- Using direct-borrow interlibrary loan options in systems such as FirstSearch or CSA

A library technology or research application may be less likely to work as an LTA when it involves large numbers of steps, combines multiple technologies, or has questionable utility for faculty or students. For example, there are times when it is useful to understand what MARC records are, but an LTA that provides a detailed explanation of them may be of questionable value.

CREATING AN LTA

Just two skills, word processing and screen-shot capture, are needed to create a basic LTA. Librarians experienced with video-capture tools (e.g., TechSmith's Camtasia or Macromedia's Captivate) may be tempted to develop more sophisticated video tutorials. For most LTAs it is best to just keep it simple. The LTA archive will provide many examples of how one is best constructed. Applying design thinking in the form of BLAAM to the process will also help. The steps in BLAAM will allow for the blending of instructional design and technology skills into our existing knowledge of library technology. Rather than simply creating tutorials, handouts, or pathfinders that we then mount on a website, we should allow our instructional design and technology influences to give us a different and more thoughtful approach to the development of resources like LTAs.

An informal assessment process is a good starting point. With limited time, it makes sense to conduct an assessment to determine what the faculty's most pressing needs are and then use that information to prioritize ideas for what can make a good LTA. Next, identify a set of objectives for the LTA's outcomes. What learning gaps should the LTA eliminate among faculty after they have used the LTA? With properly identified objectives and assessment methods, the process of evaluation and revision will be made easier. Once an LTA is in the development stage, librarians may find that working with a storyboard makes good sense for it. The basic storyboard should identify the key elements that faculty will need to learn to use the technology and lay out the steps in accomplishing the task in a logical fashion. We often take for granted the inherent complexity or confusion of our information technologies, so creating a storyboard that identifies the steps from the perspective of a completely inexperienced user will contribute to a more successful LTA. The next step is to migrate the storyboard content to a web page.

Begin with a brief introductory section that explains the LTA. Identify the benefits of the LTA and what it will help faculty members to accomplish. Stress the educational benefits by giving specific examples of how it will save faculty members time while providing an educational advantage for their students. Even better, provide a concrete example of how faculty may currently be accomplishing an educational task and indicate how and where the LTA will save time and improve results. Next, proceed with the text that will provide the actual step-by-step instructions faculty will follow. When creating the LTA on the web page, it is efficient to keep open the actual application being explained, your word processor, your screen-shot software, and the campus courseware if the LTA involves course site integration.

As you proceed through the explanation of the procedure, write the text for each step and then capture the necessary screen shot needed to illustrate the step. Any number of LTAs are enhanced with the editing and drawing tools found in screen-shot software or Microsoft Word. Use these tools to emphasize important parts of the process or to provide additional instructions within screen shots. For example, a text box and arrow combination could be used to pinpoint exactly which button must be clicked or where a URL must be added. Users of SnagIt software, which is excellent for creating the exact type of screen shots used in LTAs, makes adding arrows and text directly onto a screen shot quite easy. Perhaps the only caution to offer is that an LTA developer should avoid taking for granted that any part of the technology application being described is too obvious. Avoid assuming in advance that the target audience is going to be technologically savvy about any step in the process. Once the LTA is completed, it should go through a formative evaluation with potential users to determine if it makes sense and covers the topic well enough to resolve the targeted learning gaps. This will enable revisions and finishing touches to improve the quality of the final LTA, which can then be brought to the attention of Charles Ansorge for possible inclusion in the official LTA site.

SAMPLE DEVELOPMENT OF AN LTA: KEEPING FOUND THINGS FINDABLE

In this chapter we have focused primarily on library-related LTAs that can be used to promote the library's electronic resources as instructional technologies. But academic librarians can certainly expand their LTA development beyond the library. In fact, by demonstrating to faculty colleagues that they have mastered a range of instructional technologies and software, blended librarians can effectively promote themselves and the library as a campus technology leader. This section of the chapter will take the reader through the key steps in the process of creating an LTA, and the example is a nonlibrary technology. However, it is one with good potential to allow faculty to achieve efficiencies while also promoting useful skills such as "keeping up" for professional development and becoming more organized. We believe these are skills that would be beneficial to most faculty and that would have a high WIIFM factor.

Step One
Identifying the LTA

In the Internet age everyone is spending more time accessing information in the form of mainstream media news, professional resources, blog posts, webcasts, instructional videos, and other miscellaneous web-based content. As we tend to find more information it becomes increasingly difficult to keep track of all that information, and we find new information at such a rapid pace that we often lack time to properly store it for future reference. Because of this, faculty may come to us at one time or another with the question, "I came across something on the Web I found of interest, but now I can't find it again—can you help me find it?" Part of the challenge this particular question presents is that unless you record or store certain information as soon as you find it, it may no longer be there when you try to relocate it a month or even a week later. The good news is that there are tools to help our faculty gain efficiency in "keeping found things findable." This LTA will be designed to introduce one of the better ones and demonstrate how to use it effectively. It is advisable, before embarking on the development of an LTA, to conduct a small needs assessment to determine if the LTA is really needed and is likely to be used by the target audience.

Step Two
Setting the Objectives

For this LTA, we have identified several objectives that will both guide our development process and allow us to later determine if we achieved our intended outcomes. They are

- The learner will understand the importance of capturing web information at the time it is located and will gain an understanding of the "keep found things findable" concept.
- The learner will develop personalized strategies for keeping found things findable.

- The learner will be able to use FURL to collect, store, and retrieve information found on the Internet.
- The learner will understand FURL's ability to promote the sharing of found information.
- The learner will understand how FURL differs from other web-based bookmarking services.

Step Three
Introduction to the LTA

The first step in the development of the actual LTA would be the introduction. It should provide some background information about the LTA and indicate both the author's intentions and learning objectives. That makes step two, identifying objectives, doubly useful because it can be integrated directly into the LTA's introductory section. This LTA will be titled "Keeping Found Things Findable—An LTA for Using FURL." Here is its brief introduction:

> This page contains information on keeping found things findable and demonstrates a web-based application useful for this function. As Internet searchers access more and more information, they also tend to lose it or forget where they found it. The goal of keeping found things findable is to avoid the dreaded feeling of knowing something important has been previously found on the Internet but being unable to find it again or spending many hours in the pursuit of lost information.

This information would be followed by a brief description of FURL (a "file cabinet" for URLs) and the objectives for the LTA. Next the LTA designer would start providing step-by-step instructions for getting started with the application. These would include

1. Navigate to the home page of FURL at http://www.furl.net.
2. First-time users will need to register as a user. There is no fee for using FURL.
3. To facilitate capturing web pages to FURL, it is recommended that you download and install one of FURL's "browser buttons." Installing the button in the "Links" area of your Internet browser will make capturing web pages far easier. More about the function of the browser button will be demonstrated.
4. After installing the browser button, navigate to a web page you want to store.

Step Four
Providing Screen Shots

In addition to the textual instructions found in LTAs, there are always ample screen shots to illustrate the instructions. For example, in this LTA an instruction would need to show how to add a web page to FURL. This requires first navigating to a web page, then clicking on the FURL browser button, and then completing a template used to gather information about the web page. Rather than just explaining the procedure, it can be illustrated more powerfully with a screen shot. Figure 6-6 is an example.

Here is an example of the text that would accompany the screen shot:

> After pressing the button, a new web page will appear with this box displayed. FURL will automatically insert the title of the web page and its URL. That by itself is a time-saver. Users can specify the quality or usefulness of the page with a rating if they like. FURL has two devices for helping to find things once they are no longer easy to recall. First, there are folders—termed "topic" in the display. In this example, a new folder titled "higher education" is being created for this article. Second, FURL users can assign keywords to help describe the article for

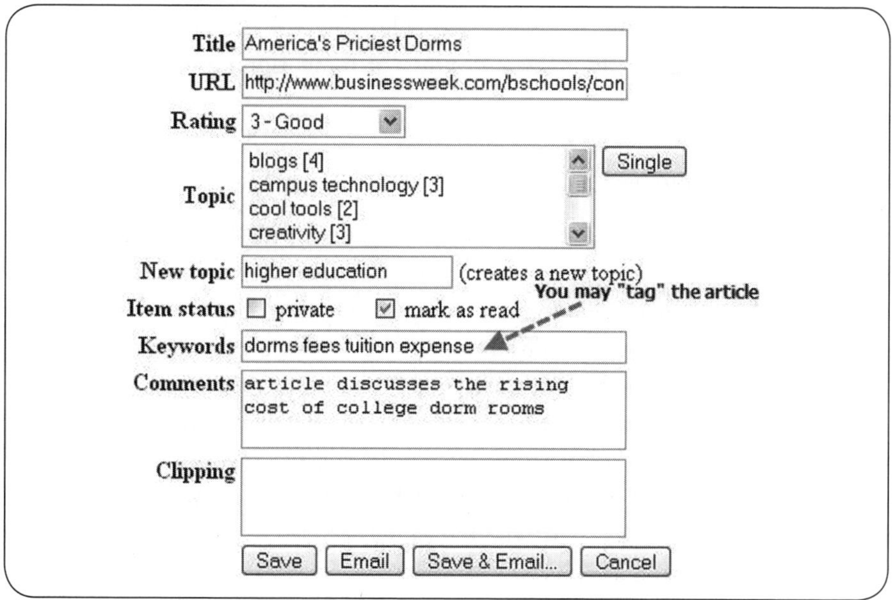

FIGURE 6-6
Sample of FURL: Adding a document

later retrieval. Finally, users can add comments about the article and even cut and paste into FURL actual content from the article. This can be useful if an important quote needs to be highlighted.

Academic librarians who want to design LTAs will need to acquire good-quality software for capturing screen shots. The Microsoft default screen-shot capture is a possibility, but software packages such as TechSmith's SnagIt are far superior. Having the ability to edit screen shots and add graphics and text to them makes it relatively simple to enhance the screen shots used in LTAs. For good examples of editing screen shots to incorporate directional graphics and texts, see the completed LTA for using FURL at http://staff.philau.edu/bells/kftf.htm.

Step Five
Completing the LTA

There is no specific guideline for how long an LTA should be, but most are not lengthy. Recall that one characteristic of an LTA is that it should take no more than thirty to sixty minutes to learn the technology described in the LTA. Keeping the LTA brief is always an asset. The challenge is to determine how much detail the LTA user is likely to need. The less text the better. If the screen shots can deliver the message graphically, that's desirable. The LTA can be completed with links to additional resources if there are any worth mentioning.

Step Six
Formative Evaluation

Once the LTA is complete, the next step from our BLAAM model would be to briefly conduct formative evaluation. This is another way of saying "get some feedback." The LTA may seem to make good sense, follow a logical order of operation, and provide clear instructions, but the LTA developer is sometimes so familiar with the technology that he or she is unable to view it from the perspective of a novice. Therefore, it is critical to have someone completely new to the technology test the LTA. This is the best way to detect faults and flaws within the LTA. Have the tester write down anything about the LTA that is unclear, both in the text and graphics. Use the comments to revise the LTA as needed.

Step Seven
Implementation and Maintenance

Once the LTA has been tested and revised, it is now ready to be made available to the library's user community. As more individuals use the LTA, it is possible that additional comments will lead to additional revisions or content. The developer may also wish to submit the LTA to the official LTA website for possible inclusion in the collection. An LTA is a dynamic instructional product. Most will require some occasional updating when enhancements to the tools covered in the LTA undergo change, such as interface enhancements. For example, the LTA that covers the use of tables of contents and alerts services needs to be updated as new services are offered by electronic information providers and as the features are changed. It can sometimes be a challenge to keep up with change and to make the necessary edits to keep the LTA up-to-date.

CONCLUSION

By themselves, LTAs will only marginally advance librarians' ability to collaborate with faculty. In the grander scheme, any number of strategies may further position the academic librarian as a partner in the teaching and learning process. Librarians can be technology leaders for their users in other library environments as well, including K–12 education, public libraries, special libraries, and in fact anywhere that basic library "teachnologies" can help our users increase their productivity and help them do a better job. Although this chapter promotes the potential of LTAs to help librarians collaborate with faculty, librarians are also encouraged to develop LTAs in cooperation with other academic support professionals, including teaching and learning center staff, writing center staff, instructional technologists, and even information technologists. Those colleagues understand and share our goal of furthering faculty collaboration. By working cooperatively we can identify and produce even better LTAs. Our faculty may be too busy for personalized technology training, but when properly designed and promoted, LTAs will further our goal of getting them to apply our "teachnologies" in education that achieves institutional outcomes.

TOPICS FOR FURTHER DISCUSSION

What ideas for LTAs that could be of use to your faculty came to mind while reading this chapter? Share your ideas for feedback and discussion with the blended librarians community.

Do you think that LTAs should also be made available to students, although they have been traditionally developed for faculty?

What software have you used to develop screen shots, and would you recommend it to other academic librarians?

If you have developed other types of instructional tutorials, how do you think they compare to LTAs? Do you think an LTA can be as effective as a tutorial that is created with more sophisticated tools? Do you think LTAs are less effective because they don't offer the interaction or feedback mechanisms of more sophisticated digital learning materials?

ADDITIONAL RESOURCES

Calhoun, Terry. 2004. "LTAs—Replacements for the Missing 'Professional Development.'" *Syllabus News* (March 11). http://www.campus-technology.com/news_article.asp?id=9077&typeid=153.

Carrington, Allan. 2003. "Retooling for Creative Curriculum: Using Low Threshold Activities to Produce Best Practice Educational Multimedia and Hypermedia." http://www.unity.com.au/LTApaper/paper.html.

Starret, David. 2005. "LTAs to the Rescue." *Campus Technology* 18 (April): 48–49.

7 Digital Learning Materials

Enhancing the Instructional Role of Librarians

Libraries must be part of the fabric of the new electronic infrastructure that is emerging. Access to the content, the services, and the organization of information is essential to teaching, learning, and inquiry at all levels of the educational systems, as well as to society at large.

—Brian Hawkins, president of Educause

OBJECTIVES

1. Identify what digital learning materials (DLMs) are.
2. Identify the benefits of DLMs to the institution and its library.
3. Identify the different means by which DLMs can by located.
4. Explain the various methods by which librarians can utilize DLMs to enhance instruction.

A RESOURCE FOR TEACHING AND LEARNING

Digital learning materials are quickly becoming an integral resource that faculty and students use to enhance the teaching and learning process. This chapter will look at what DLMs are, why they are useful in enhancing student learning, what role librarians can play in helping to locate and use DLMs, how librarians can create and use DLMs to enhance library instruction, and some possible future directions for DLMs.

This chapter builds on previous chapters' discussion of design principles and instructional technology. While reading this chapter and thinking about various approaches that libraries can take to locate, create, and utilize DLMs, it is essential not to divorce the process from learner analysis and instructional design (ADDIE or BLAAM) in order to better integrate the library into the learning process and help faculty and students learn about information literacy and library services and resources.

LETTING GO OF LEARNING OBJECTS TO EMBRACE DIGITAL LEARNING MATERIALS

In the past decade, the breadth and depth of digital information have exploded. Technologies now exist that allow information to be digitized and made accessible to a worldwide audience quickly, easily, and inexpensively. The resulting tidal wave of digital information makes it challenging for faculty, students, and librarians to keep up with the deluge of digital resources in the information age. Just in the last decade digital learning materials have experienced tremendous growth, and they are poised to dramatically affect higher education in the next decade by enhancing courses that make use of Internet technologies (i.e., course/learning management systems) to share digital course resources.

While some types of DLMs are frequently used by faculty, students, and librarians in higher education, they remain mostly on the fringes of the digital materials that are sought after by faculty to enhance their courses. There are several reasons for this. First, the library profession for the most part has not embraced the role of collector, organizer, and disseminator of DLMs, even though they are related to materials that audiovisual and media libraries have been collecting for several decades. Second, the market for DLMs is only now beginning to mature enough so that commercial vendors see the potential economic rewards in creating and selling them. Additionally, because DLMs are relatively new to higher education and are more complex than traditional print materials like books or journals, they can be difficult to distinguish from similar or related types of digital educational materials such as learning objects, informational objects, instructional objects, and multimedia teaching objects.

It is not surprising, then, that there is a great deal of disagreement and contention in the scholarly community over the definition of these terms. In order to provide a more detailed context to the definition, this chapter will briefly touch upon this debate. Most important, by choosing to use the term *digital learning materials* instead of the other terms mentioned previously, this chapter seeks to provide a definition that can encompass the other terms that have narrower definitions but is not so broad that its definition is rendered meaningless.

DEFINING DLMS

The most common of the aforementioned terms is *learning object.* However, this term is also the most contentious and highly debated one. The following is a brief excerpt from Shank's article "The Emergence of Learning Objects: The Reference Librarian's Role."

> One widely cited general definition, from the Learning Object Metadata Working Group of the IEEE Learning Technology Standards Committee (2001), is "any entity, digital or non-digital, which can be used, re-used or referenced during technology supported learning" (2002, Section 1.1, 1). This definition is extremely vague and much of the literature (Friesen, 2003, Polsani, 2003, and Shepherd, 2000) asserts that it is too broad a definition to be meaningful. David Merrill (2002) explains that "as usually defined learning objects are of little use to anyone." Consequently, many of the stakeholders have taken different directions in their attempt to define a learning object, which has led to the creation of various definitions that are tied to the primary interests and concerns of their proponents (Rehak and Mason 2003). David Wiley (2000) states that "the proliferation of definitions for the term 'learning object' makes communication confusing and difficult." (Shank 2003)

The term *digital learning materials* attempts to sidestep this debate and make communication about these types of materials less confusing for librarians and instructors. The term *digital learning materials,* or *DLMs,* is useful as an umbrella to encompass these other, narrower terms. A DLM can be defined simply as *any interactive web-based digital resource that is used for instruction.* To further clarify what DLMs are, it is useful to pull apart the various components that make up the definition of a DLM. The key components of the definition can be separated as follows:

- a web-based digital resource
- interactive
- used for instruction (i.e., instructional)

A web-based digital resource can use any of the following types of file formats: HTML, JavaScript, SWF, AVI, WMV, MP3, WAV, JPEG, and TIFF, as well as many other existing types. This means that DLMs are comprised of multimedia components such as text, graphics, animation, audio, and video, though not all of these multimedia components need be present.

The next important component of a DLM is that it has interactivity built in. This means that digital learning materials can come in such forms as tutorials, simulations, educational games, demonstrations, exercises, experiments, adaptive learning modules, and case studies. A DLM does not have to include all kinds of interactivity, but it should include some components such as exercises, quizzing, games, simulations, or some other kind of task that might involve text entry, drag and drop, multiple select, or button pushing and thus require the learner to interact with the material presented.

The final component of a DLM is that it can be used in an instructional process. The DLM must have some aspect of assessment included so that the learner can get synchronous or asynchronous feedback on the activities he or she is participating in, thereby promoting student learning of a concept or set of concepts. This feedback may or may not be recorded and viewable by an instructor.

There are a great number of library tutorials that qualify as DLMs. The following are a few examples of these.

- Texas Information Literacy Tutorial (TILT; http://tilt.lib.utsystem.edu)
- Plagiarism and Academic Integrity Simulation (http://www.scc.rutgers.edu/douglass/sal/plagiarism/intro.html)
- Boolean Operators Tutorial (http://library.nyu.edu/research/tutorials/boolean/boolean.html)

To help make DLMs more concrete, it is useful to more closely examine one of the aforementioned examples. The Boolean Operators Tutorial created by the Bobst Library of New York University is an excellent example of a DLM because it has all of the aforementioned components. It focuses on enhancing the learner's understanding of Boolean operators and their use in searching library databases.

This tutorial contains various instructional components, including a research problem with assignment, various associated learning activities, and related assessment feedback. The learning activities are a series of exercises related to the research assignment (in the hypothetical assignment, students are asked to present evidence supporting the theory that the government has concealed alien or UFO encounters), with the intent of enabling the learner to gain experience using Boolean operators through repeated practice. As the learner proceeds through the tutorial, it provides immediate feedback to each of the answers the student chooses. This helps the learner gain a deeper understanding of how to apply the searching concepts. (See figure 7-1.) Besides containing activities such as multiple-choice questions, this tutorial also includes animations that depict the concepts of Boolean operators.

DLMS ENCOURAGE GOOD PRACTICE

The best method for understanding how DLMs can enhance the teaching and learning process is to use Chickering and Ehrmann's "Implementing the Seven Principles: Technology as Lever" as a context for demonstrating this. Their article discusses the seven instructional practices that are necessary in order for technology to be most effective in enhancing learning. The seven principles are

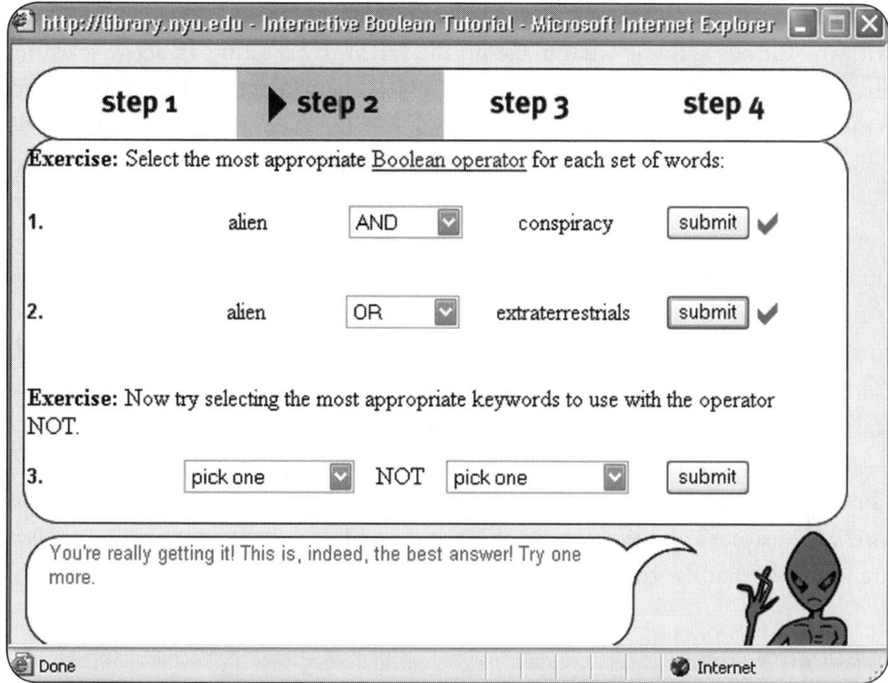

FIGURE 7-1

Questions from the Bobst Library's Boolean Operators Tutorial

1. Good practice encourages contacts between students and faculty.
2. Good practice develops reciprocity and cooperation among students.
3. Good practice uses active learning techniques.
4. Good practice gives prompt feedback.
5. Good practice emphasizes time on task.
6. Good practice communicates high expectations.
7. Good practice respects diverse talents and ways of learning.

There are four of the seven principles that digital learning materials most promote by their use, and these are as follows: uses active learning techniques, gives prompt feedback, emphasizes time on task, and respects diverse talents and ways of learning.

Active Learning

One of the greatest benefits of using DLMs is that they allow the learner to experience the topic or concepts that are being presented to them. This type of simulated experience provides authentic opportunities for the learner to interact with the various activities that make up the DLM. By creating an active learning environment, the DLM enhances and facilitates the student's ability to learn and retain the material. This type of experiential learning is considered by many to be one of the most effective methods for assisting students in the learning process.

As mentioned previously, there are many different formats that DLMs can use such as simulations, tutorials, games, interactive exercises, and so on, but all of these formats help to stimulate and engage the learner. This means that the learner is no longer limited to passively reading or watching the information presented to them but is expected to interact with the topic or concepts being presented. Additionally, the learner is challenged by the various activities to demonstrate a learned competency with the presented material.

The Bobst Library's Boolean Operators Tutorial is a good example for blended librarians to study because it uses a number of different exercises to engage and assess the learner's ability to apply effective searching skills. The types of exercises are varied so that the tutorial is not too repetitive for the learner.

Feedback

Another powerful benefit that DLMs offer is the ability to test and provide immediate feedback to the learner. They do this by pointing out to learners their own strengths and weaknesses in how well they understand the material. Some DLMs are designed so that the learner has to master a particular idea or concept before he or she can progress. This constructivist dynamic enables learners to be more self-directed and responsible for their own learning of the material.

In addition to testing the learners as they move through the DLM, some of these materials incorporate both pre- and postassessment. There are several advantages to including both pre- and postassessment in the material. First, learners benefit when they are able to receive feedback from the postassessment so that they can learn from their mistakes. DLMs can also be composed so that learners have to achieve a certain level of mastery before they can complete the DLM, thereby ensuring that upon successful completion the learners have acquired the needed skills or knowledge. Second, DLMs can provide useful feedback and assessment to the instructor. The instructor knows that students who successfully complete a DLM are at approximately the same level of understanding. This can allow the instructor to spend more time interacting and discussing the material with students instead of simply lecturing and exposing the students to it. The instructor can also see how effective the DLM is at helping the learners understand the material by comparing the pre- and postassessments.

The Bobst Library's Boolean Operators Tutorial is admittedly not a perfect example of a DLM. It does not include a pre- and postassessment, but by coupling the DLM with a course management system, a pre- and postassessment could be created that would demonstrate the learner's success at mastering the searching skills and concepts. Also, this tutorial does not force the learner to master the material in order to progress through it; rather, it allows the learner to navigate around in the tutorial, be self-directed, and move nonlinearly through the material.

Time on Task

DLMs can also motivate learners to increase the amount of time they spend learning the topic or concepts that are presented. This benefit should not be underestimated. One of the primary factors in students' success within a particular course is the time they spend engaged with the course content. DLMs have the potential to encourage students to engage more deeply with their studies and increase the amount of time they spend on the course material.

Unlike a textbook or course reading, DLMs when integrated into a course management system like Blackboard can provide the instructor with information about the amount of time that a student has spent using the DLM. While this cannot tell the instructor about the quality of the time spent, it does record whether the student has made any effort to use the DLM. Additionally, as previously mentioned, the activities and testing in some DLMs are set up so that the learner cannot progress or complete the DLM unless he or she successfully masters each section of it.

Finally, DLMs allow learners to move at their own pace. Consequently, students who are more knowledgeable about the material can progress rapidly through the content, while students who are less skilled can take as much time as they need to review the material.

Diverse Ways of Learning

Students demonstrate a diverse number of learning styles. DLMs are beneficial because of their ability to address these different styles of learning. Most DLMs contain more than just static text; they typically include audio and visual content, which appeals to the new generation of learners who have grown up with television and the Internet.

The Bobst Library's Boolean Operators Tutorial does include both text and animation but lacks audio. Consequently, this tutorial will most appeal to learners who enjoy reading or who are visual learners, but it could be of less interest to those who are aural learners. It is not always necessary to create or use DLMs that appeal to every type of learning style, but owing to their multimedia elements, DLMs will typically meet the needs of multiple learning-style formats.

A NEEDLE IN A HAYSTACK: LOCATING DLMS

One of the main reasons why digital learning materials are adopted less frequently by faculty when compared to other instructional technologies is the difficulty in locating existing DLMs. Unlike traditional library materials such as books and periodicals, DLMs do not have semantically consistent metadata that allows them to be effortlessly searched across various repositories. Librarians (i.e., cataloging or metadata) could play an important role in helping to create the metadata structures that would allow them to successfully catalog these materials for traditional library catalogs. Additionally, librarians could partner with their institutions and existing repositories to assist in this process.

Rather than discuss how librarians could help in developing systems that allow DLMs to be cataloged, stored, and effectively retrieved, our focus is on how librarians, in the current environment, can help faculty to locate useful DLMs. Since a primary functionality of all learning objects is to offer some degree of flexibility in their use, it is often a good idea to seek out an existing DLM that can be reused as is or adapted to a new learning objective before developing a DLM from scratch. Public services librarians (i.e., reference, instruction) can and should play an active role in helping faculty to find and use digital libraries, repositories, and "referitories" (this term was coined by Carl Berger and means that the online index or database only links to the DLMs and does not store them) where they can locate relevant, high-quality DLMs.

In the current environment, instructors need the assistance of librarians (and their search skills and knowledge) more than ever to locate DLMs. There are currently a number of institutions in higher education, as well as nonprofit and public organizations and companies, that have or are creating digital learning material libraries, repositories, and referitories. They all have very different search interfaces, in addition to collecting DLMs for various disciplines. Faculty work under stressful time constraints, and therefore it is no surprise they would gravitate to DLMs that are included as supplemental material with the textbooks they use. While some of these DLMs are useful and of high quality, it is likely that these faculty are overlooking dozens of potentially useful DLMs simply because there is no easy way to locate them. Since cataloging DLMs is still in its infancy, it can be very time-consuming and challenging to locate appropriate DLMs. Librarians can assist faculty by proactively identifying relevant repositories and referitories or by training instructors on how to quickly and efficiently search the online databases; or librarians can encourage faculty to contact them and ask the librarians to take the time to locate relevant DLMs.

Criteria Used in Locating Appropriate DLMs

There are a number of important considerations for locating relevant digital learning materials. Just as when searching a library database for an article, it is important to first consider the relevant subject or topic sought, in conjunction with the kind of resources desired. The next step is to identify the most appropriate repositories and referitories in which to start the search. Figure 7-2 shows the important criteria that should be considered when searching for relevant DLMs.

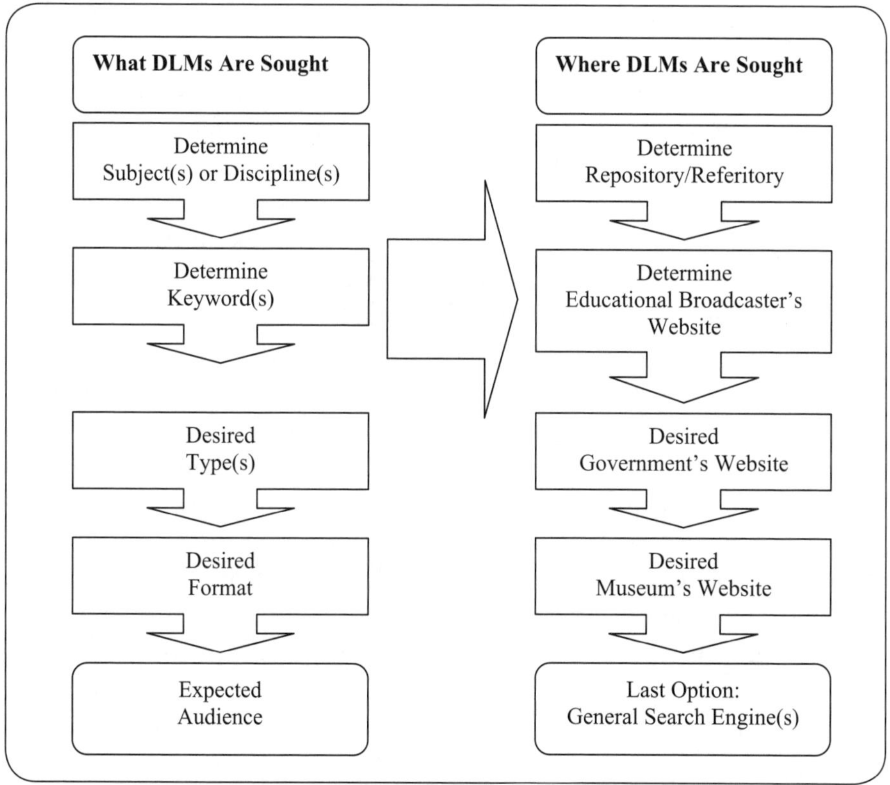

FIGURE 7-2

DLM search criteria steps

Most repositories and referitories make use of different organizational schemes, and this can make it difficult to identify the subject or discipline of the material within a particular repository or referitory. However, many repositories and referitories do provide a browse function based on their particular schema. Using this tool can be quite useful in narrowing down the search to a specific subset of the type of DLM that is wanted.

Nevertheless, locating a particular type of DLM in a referitory remains challenging. Let's consider a search to locate a DLM about Boolean operators. Here's how it would work in the MERLOT general referitory. It is possible to click on the browse function and follow subject categories starting with "Education," then look under "Library and Information Services," and finally get to "Information Retrieval." However, this pathway will not locate a DLM on Boolean operators. Rather, it is necessary to first look under the subject heading "Science and Technology," then under "Information Technology," and finally arrive at "Information Literacy," which has the Bobst Library's Boolean Operators Tutorial. This example demonstrates one of the shortcomings of the classification schemes used by repositories and referitories.

Because the classification schemes of the various repositories and referitories can differ so widely, it is also important to create a list of synonymous keywords. It is useful to identify a few relevant keywords or phrases that describe the material sought after because quite often this is more effective in quickly retrieving the relevant DLM. In the aforementioned example, if the keyword *Boolean* is typed into the basic "search materials" box, the Bobst Library's Boolean Operators Tutorial is quickly retrieved. However, it is also possible using this method to exclude resources that do not list the chosen keyword in the DLM's item record.

There are several other crucial components to locating the most appropriate DLMs for an instructor. These include identifying the type in addition to the format of the DLM desired. The type of DLM refers to the medium of the resource, such as games, interactive animations, simulations, web-based tutorials, or multimedia presentations. The next section of this chapter will examine how to determine the type of DLM preferred for a specific learning activity. The format of the DLM refers to the technologies that it is composed of and that are utilized by the resource. The format can include but is not limited to such technologies as Flash, Authorware, JavaScript, MP3, or QuickTime. The format often determines what software will be needed in order to view and use the digital learning material.

Lastly, just as some textbooks are geared for college-level courses instead of high school–level courses, it is necessary to determine the appropriateness of the DLM for the students it is intended for. Many repositories and referitories will allow the searcher to narrow and focus the search to a specified educational level.

However, if using a search engine, it is not possible to select a delimiter based on educational level, and therefore it is necessary to either use a keyword phrase or limit the domain of the search to a specific educational institution.

Where to Locate Appropriate DLMs

Once the subject matter along with the type, format, and audience level of the desired DLM are clearly defined, it is necessary to select the starting place to conduct the search. While this is not always an easy process (see figure 7-2), quite often the best place to start is with a general repository or referitory, since they are more focused on collecting digital learning materials. As previously mentioned, repositories house the DLMs, while referitories link or point to the resources housed elsewhere. This means that repositories have the advantage of directly controlling the resources they index, while referitories must frequently update their DLM records to avoid broken and obsolete links.

Many repositories and referitories have both a browse and a search function. Quite often they will include both a simple keyword search tool and more advanced searching features. One of the most important factors in facilitating a quick search is determining the right repository or referitory to start with. Besides general repositories and referitories (e.g., Wisconsin Online, MERLOT, and LOLA), there are also discipline-specific ones (e.g., iLumina and SMETE).

One of the most venerable and best-known general referitories is MERLOT. It describes itself as "a free and open resource designed primarily for faculty and students of higher education" (http://www.merlot.org). This referitory includes links to online learning materials along with additional metadata such as annotations, which include peer reviews and assignments. Because MERLOT's collection is so large and varied, it is important to have both the type and format of digital learning material clearly defined. MERLOT includes both a simple keyword search and a complex search interface. Additionally, it is possible (as demonstrated in the previous example) to browse the referitory through MERLOT's own subject indexing terms. MERLOT is not the only referitory; see table 7-1 for a more complete list.

One high-quality repository is the Wisconsin Online Resource Center. This repository is created and maintained by the Wisconsin Technical College System. It allows faculty within this system to create and store their digital learning materials, but anyone can view, link to, and utilize these DLMs. The quality of DLMs is very high because Wisconsin Online has criteria that must be met in order for DLMs to be housed in its repository. This repository includes only a simple keyword search. However, it is possible to browse the repository through its own subject indexing terms.

TABLE 7-1

DLM repositories and referitories

Repository	Description
MERLOT Multimedia Educational Resource for Learning and Online Teaching http://www.merlot.org	One of the largest and oldest multidisciplinary collections of DLMs available
Wisconsin Online Resource Center http://www.wisc-online.com	A multidisciplinary collection of learning objects for the state's 16 technical colleges
LOLA Exchange Learning Objects, Learning Activities http://www.lolaexchange.org	A multidisciplinary collection of high-quality learning objects for Wesleyan College
iLumina Educational Resources for Science and Mathematics http://www.ilumina-dlib.org	A collection of teaching materials for chemistry, biology, physics, mathematics, and computer science
SMETE Science, Mathematics, Engineering, and Technology Education http://www.smete.org	A collection of science, mathematics, engineering, and technology teaching and learning materials for all educational levels
PRIMO Peer-Reviewed Instructional Materials Online http://www.ala.org/ala/acrlbucket/is/iscommittees/webpages/emergingtech/primo/index.htm	A database of instructional materials for discovering, accessing, and evaluating information online

While repositories and referitories are good starting points for searching for DLMs, there are several other locations on the Internet that can be profitable when trying to locate them. Educational entertainment websites can be very useful in locating DLMs. Some examples of these sites are the Public Broadcasting Service (PBS), The Learning Channel, The History Channel, and National Geographic. Because these media broadcasters are in the business of developing educational print and media resources, they have the assets to also develop high-quality DLMs. Over the past decade they have started to create interactive online multimedia resources in conjunction with their programming. A large portion of the DLMs that these broadcasters create are geared for the K–12 market. However, there are still a large number of DLMs that higher education can utilize, though it is important to pay attention to the intended audience when making selections.

The DLMs that these broadcasters have created are accessible from their websites. A good way to locate DLMs at these sites is to visit the place that is created specially for teachers (generally K–12). This location provides access to teaching materials, supplements, and resources related to the broadcaster's programming. Additionally, it is possible to search by topic within current or archived programming. Once an appropriate program is found, it will often provide links to additional resources or teaching materials, which in turn may point to useful digital materials. Finally, many of the sites offer a simple keyword search. Because it is a basic keyword search, it can be challenging to locate specific DLMs. It is often more productive to use the keyword search to locate the programming related to the desired DLM and then follow the process stated above.

Government and museum websites are also useful locations that can be searched to locate DLMs. These organizations have begun producing educational, interactive, web-based, multimedia resources over the past few years. For example, the National Aeronautics and Space Administration (NASA) produces numerous resources for K–12 teachers, and some of the materials would be appropriate for undergraduates learning about physics and astronomy. Similarly, the Museum of Modern Art (New York) has created resources to educate the public about art history, and some of these resources would be useful for those studying art. Like the aforementioned broadcaster sites, government and museum sites can be searched in the same manner, by using both basic keyword and advanced search tools, as well as by going to the section developed for teachers, when it is an option. To meet with the greatest success, it is important to use subject-relevant government and museum sites.

Lastly, Internet search engines can be used to locate digital learning materials. Search engines should not be ignored, because it is possible to locate very useful and appropriate learning objects through them that would not have been found through any other means, but they should be viewed as a last option when all other means to locate a DLM have failed. This is because it takes a great deal more time and effort to locate DLMs when using search engines.

Search engines (i.e., Google, AlltheWeb, AltaVista, MSN, Yahoo!, etc.) offer both simple and various types of more advanced keyword search tools. When searching for a DLM, use the advanced search tools. Because search engines have various advanced search tools, it is not possible to create a "one size fits all" approach to using them to locate a DLM. Generally, it is best to use the largest search engines such as Google, MSN, AlltheWeb, and AltaVista.

Finally, to be successful in locating DLMs using search engines, it is important to follow the steps below:

1. Search using the identified keywords that relate to the subject or name of the DLM.
2. Add keywords that refer to the type of DLM desired (i.e., tutorial, simulation, game, module, etc.).
3. If possible, identify and limit according to the format of the DLM sought (i.e., Flash, JavaScript, AVI, etc.).
4. Search specific location domains such as .org, .edu, or .gov (or you can identify specific locations such as PBS, Penn State University, or NASA).
5. It may be advantageous to search for DLMs within a specific time range (such as searching within the past year to identify the most up-to-date material).

UTILIZING DLMS: THE IFDEE MODEL

Academic librarians can certainly apply their searching skills in locating DLMs, but once they are discovered, librarians must be able to successfully use DLMs in their instruction. It is important to remember the ADDIE and BLAAM models when designing any instructional process. However, we suggest a slightly different model for integrating and employing DLMs. This is the IFDEE (identify, find, develop, employ, and evaluate) model.

It is important to remember that when using DLMs, the focus should be on the learning and not on the technology. Therefore, the first and most important step (identify) in successfully integrating DLMs into instruction is to consider the students' needs and the goals and objectives of the class or instruction session. If there is an identifiable gap in the students' understanding of a particular topic or concept because they are unable to meet specified goals or objectives, a DLM on that subject may help the students gain a better understanding of the material. Additionally, librarians may want to take advantage of the fact that DLMs allow students to be exposed to a topic or concept prior to the instruction occurring face-to-face. Allowing all students exposure to the material prior to class gives them an opportunity to interact with the librarian (instructor) in a more knowledgeable state. The key to the "identify" step is to determine where the gaps in student learning are so that a DLM addressing that specific student need can be employed. For example, in the Bobst Library's Boolean Operators Tutorial, students who are struggling to understand how to use Boolean search operators can have additional exposure and practice with the concept.

The second phase (find) in utilizing DLMs is being able to locate the appropriate DLM that matches the identified learning need. It is in this phase that you follow the search procedure that was explained in the previous section. Remember to follow these steps:

- Identify what DLM is appropriate and search using
  - Subject/discipline heading
  - Keywords
  - Type
  - Format
  - Audience
- Identify where the DLM resides by
  - Repository/referitory libraries or databases
  - Educational entertainment sites
  - Professional organization sites
  - Government sites
  - Search engines

The third phase (develop) involves developing strategies for integrating the DLM into the course. This entails deciding how to have the students access the DLM. For example, it is possible to link to or import a DLM directly into a course management system such as Blackboard. Additionally, it is important to consider the instructional activities of the DLM and decide how to enhance it. For example, if the Bobst Library's Boolean Operators Tutorial is linked to a Blackboard course, then a librarian could create a simple quiz that the students would have to complete after taking the DLM to demonstrate their mastery of the concept.

The fourth phase (employ) deals with making use of the DLM in the course. There are several factors to consider when deciding to employ a DLM. First, determine if the DLM should be used inside or outside the classroom. If using it in the classroom, will it serve as the primary or only a supplemental means by which the students are introduced to the subject? If using the DLM outside the classroom, will it be used prior to or after the instruction session? Here is a simple checklist to consider when employing DLMs:

- Inside or outside of class
- Before, during, or after class
- As a primary or supplemental instructional tool

The final phase (evaluate) involves evaluating the effectiveness of the DLM. This is a vital step, because if the DLM is not improving student learning, then it is not accomplishing its intended goal and should either be eliminated or replaced by another, more effective DLM. Additionally, it is important to know what it is that you are measuring or assessing in order to determine the effectiveness of the DLM.

THE FUTURE OF DLMS

Prognosticating about the future is always difficult, but technologies challenge us to keep up with and adapt to the societal paradigms they enable and affect. Digital learning materials are such a technology. As DLMs mature and the issues affecting their creation, storage, and use become less of a barrier to faculty adoption, librarians need to be at the forefront of incorporating DLMs into their collections and using them in their instruction.

While some librarians have played an active role on their campuses in using and promoting DLMs, more librarians must realize that these materials are yet another digital form of information that libraries must locate, store, and share. Doing so will help libraries establish greater connections with faculty and students in the teaching and learning process. DLMs offer another opportunity for librarians to strengthen the ties they have with faculty and increase the profession's visibility and relevance to the academic community.

TOPICS FOR FURTHER DISCUSSION

What is the best way to refer to digital learning materials?

What are the different ways in which libraries can play an important role in locating, collecting, sharing, and using DLMs?

What is the best way to locate DLMs?

What is the best way to use DLMs to enhance librarian instruction?

ADDITIONAL RESOURCES

Friesen, Norm. 2003. "Three Objections to Learning Objects and E-Learning Standards." Draft version of a paper published in *Online Education Using Learning Objects,* ed. R. McGreal, 59–70. London: Routledge, 2004. http://www.learningspaces.org/n/papers/objections.html.

Institute of Electrical and Electronics Engineers, Learning Technology Standards Committee. 2001. "Draft Standard for Learning Object Metadata, Version 6.1." http://ltsc.ieee.org.ezaccess.libraries.psu.edu/doc/wg12/LOM_WD6-1_1.pdf.

Merrill, David. 2002. "Position Statement and Questions on Learning Objects Research and Practice." Paper presented at panel, "Learning Objects Technology: Implications for Educational Research and Practice," American Educational Research Association, New Orleans, April 1–5. http://www.learndev.org/LearningObjectsAERA2002.html.

Morley, B., and K. Reifman. 2003. "Boolean Operators Tutorial." Bobst Library, New York University. http://library.nyu.edu/research/tutorials/boolean/boolean.html.

Polsani, P. R. 2003. "Use and Abuse of Reusable Learning Objects." *Journal of Digital Information* 3, no. 4 (February 19). http://jodi.ecs.soton.ac.uk/Articles/v03/i04/Polsani/.

Rehak, Daniel R., and Robin Mason. 2003. "Keeping the Learning in Learning Objects." In *Reusing Online Resources: A Sustainable Approach to ELearning*, ed. A. Littlejohn. London: Kogan.

Shank, John. 2005. "Why Digital Learning Materials Matter." *NetConnect* (Fall): 16–19. http://www.libraryjournal.com/article/CA6269281.html.

Shepherd, Clive. 2000. "Objects of Interest." http://www.fastrak-consulting.co.uk/tactix/Features/objects/objects.htm.

Wiley, David A. 2000. "Connecting Learning Objects to Instructional Design Theory: A Definition, a Metaphor, and a Taxonomy." Online version: "The Instructional Use of Learning Objects." http://reusability.org/read/chapters/wiley.doc.

8 | The Blended Librarians Online Learning Community

Learning and Practicing Academic Librarianship by Design

The purpose of learning is growth, and our minds, unlike our bodies, can continue growing as we continue to live. —Mortimer Adler

OBJECTIVES

1. Summarize what the Blended Librarians Online Learning Community (BLC) is.
2. Explain the various means by which the BLC assists librarians in professional development.
3. Identify the benefits and challenges of the BLC.

A VIRTUAL PLACE TO LEARN AND GROW

In this book we have introduced more than a few new concepts: blended librarianship, library design thinking, BLAAM, A_FLIP, DLMs, and LTAs, to name a few. We believe they will provide valuable ideas for further integrating your academic library into the parent institution's teaching and learning process. However, there is no "one size fits all" model. There are significant differences between small and large, and private and public, colleges and universities across our country. Additionally, each institution has its own unique culture, and no single model or method will apply equally well to all; local customization is usually necessary. But we believe that the concepts discussed in this book should be shared and discussed among as many librarians, faculty, and support staff as possible in order to further accomplish the goal we set forth when we established the principles and practices of blended librarianship.

When we discussed how we could transform blended librarianship beyond our initial article and move from mere words on paper to concrete strategies that librarians could use to transform themselves and maintain the relevance of their libraries, we were practicing what we preach—design thinking. Our plans called for a venue that would be accessible to everyone, where people could come together to learn and share ideas about blended librarianship—in other words, a web portal that would allow anyone to learn more about blended librarianship. We also applied design thinking to create a sustainable community where librarians could learn more about blended librarianship and have opportunities to acquire the new skills needed for this new role.

This required us to assess the demand for such a community, to design a framework around which it would be developed, to develop or identify a technology and communication infrastructure that would support our design, to prototype and test our design, and then to engage our colleagues in the community so that we could learn from their experiences in making further improvements to this community of blended librarians. This process took us through several stages of design and development:

- Communicating with colleagues about our idea for a blended librarians learning community
- Researching the components of learning communities and understanding how they achieve sustainability
- Identifying an appropriate technology infrastructure to support a learning community
- Configuring a website to serve as a portal for blended librarianship and a gateway to the learning community
- Identifying key partners who would help build the community and later serve on an advisory board
- Developing a strategy to use discussion boards and resource areas as a way to get community members to engage with each other and contribute to the community
- Identifying a model for delivering ongoing continuing education events that would offer quality programming to community members

In this chapter, which focuses on the Blended Librarians Online Learning Community (BLC), we will discuss how we moved from our initial design thinking to actually developing and building a community for our colleagues who desired to learn more about blended librarianship and integrate it into their own professional practice. Here we will explore how the BLC contributes to the profession through professional development, the sharing of ideas, and the further development of the blended librarian concept. We will cover the benefits and challenges of this online community and the virtual learning that takes place there. Since collaboration is critical to blended librarianship, we will identify the ways in which we partnered with colleagues to make this project work; achieving it required help from others. Finally, we will assert that the BLC is an important means by which librarians can further their own professional development and acquire additional skill sets (i.e., design thinking, instructional design and technology).

FINDING THE RIGHT COMMUNITY INFRASTRUCTURE

The rapid pace of change in information technologies challenges the relevance of the services offered by the modern academic library. However, if used properly, advances in information technologies can allow the library to become more relevant and play a larger role in the teaching and learning process in higher education. Throughout this book, we have shared our ideas about how to use blended librarianship to enhance the library's relevance by capitalizing on design thinking and instructional technologies to further the library's integration into the classroom, both physical and virtual.

Our ideas about blended librarianship expressed in this book and elsewhere have only just begun to engage librarians in thinking about blended librarianship as a way to shape the future of their libraries. For blended librarianship to play an essential role in helping libraries stay relevant in the future, it must continue to evolve. And for it to evolve in a meaningful way, people (i.e., librarians, faculty, and support staff) who care about these issues must come together and have the opportunity to share and learn from one another.

Fortunately the Internet, along with other communication technologies, had advanced to the point where we were able to partner with a company (LearningTimes) that could provide the necessary software and infrastructure to support our goal. As described in chapter 1, the webcast workshop series sponsored by the Teaching, Learning, and Technology Group in conjunction with the Association of College and Research Libraries led to the partnerships we formed with Steven Gilbert of TLT and Hope Kandel of the LearningTimes Network, and as a result, with the support of LearningTimes we were able to establish the Blended Librarians Online Learning Community. The first community members were the attendees of the workshop (about eighty people).

Initially, we wanted the community to be a place where participants could discuss blended librarian–related issues as well as explore new ideas, share useful resources, and continue to learn from one another. Over the next two years, the community grew and evolved as we offered more TLT/ACRL-sponsored workshops, began a blended librarian webcast series, and created an advisory board. We realized that in order to sustain and grow the community, it was vital to get members involved in it. We created an advisory board to help us brainstorm ways to get members involved. The advisory board has been invaluable by helping to put into action the following initiatives:

- Asking for community members to volunteer to assist with the blended librarians website, facilitating discussion forums, and summarizing webcasts
- Planning webcast presentations
- Advertising the BLC with "Are you blended?" pins

Today the community has existed for a little over two years and has more than 2,000 members from all over the United States, as well as several other countries. The BLC offers numerous opportunities for professional development through webcast presentations, workshops, discussion forums, meeting rooms, file repositories, synchronous chats, voice boards, survey polls, and recorded archives. It is these activities that have allowed the community to grow and the concept of the blended librarian to evolve.

WHAT HAPPENS IN THE COMMUNITY

The LearningTimes Library Online Community, or LearningTimes LOC, provides the venue by which the members of the BLC can come together to share ideas and learn. There are a number of features, both synchronous and asynchronous, that a community member can use. These features include sharing images and bios, live and archived webcasts, discussion forums, polls, an online file cabinet, resource lists, instant messaging and text chat, and a virtual meeting room. All of these features contribute to the development and growth of the community. The following section will examine in detail the various tools and their uses.

Images and Bios

The images and bios section of the LearningTimes LOC allows members who join the BLC to post biographical information as well as related media (i.e., pictures, audio files, video files, Flash files). Members are encouraged to share their personal and professional information and learn more about other members in an asynchronous virtual environment. This allows members to get acquainted with each other without directly contacting and interacting with other members of the community.

This has both advantages and disadvantages. Members who are shy or less outgoing may feel empowered to share information about themselves that they might not otherwise have shared if they were in a face-to-face environment. However, because the environment is asynchronous, it is not always easy to form personal relationships and strong connections with other members of the community. This is because it is not possible to directly contact and communicate with other members unless they specifically list contact information.

Live and Archived Webcasts

The BLC also offers live webcasts through the LearningTimes LOC, which uses Elluminate Live virtual classroom software (see figure 8-1). This package allows the BLC to invite speakers to present in an online, live collaborative environment. To make these presentations as high quality as possible, we require presenters to use a practice classroom prior to giving their presentation online. This helps presenters get more comfortable with the technologies they will be using, as well as allowing us the opportunity to share the "best practices" we have learned through our extensive use of webcasting technologies. We feel that these training sessions help prepare our presenters to deliver the high-quality webcasts that members of our community expect.

Some of the more useful features of the webcasting technologies include a VoIP communications system that allows participants to converse using micro-

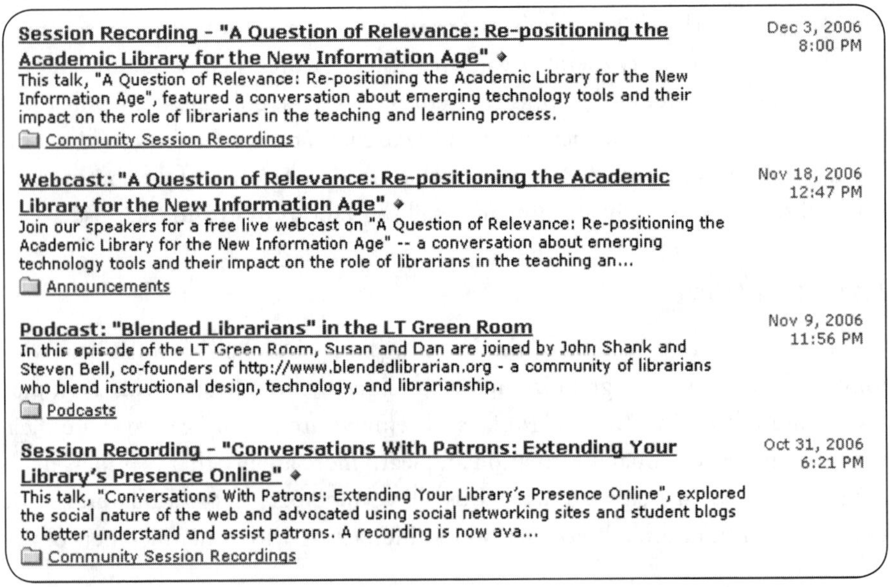

Session Recording - "A Question of Relevance: Re-positioning the Academic Library for the New Information Age" ◆ — Dec 3, 2006 8:00 PM
This talk, "A Question of Relevance: Re-positioning the Academic Library for the New Information Age", featured a conversation about emerging technology tools and their impact on the role of librarians in the teaching and learning process.
Community Session Recordings

Webcast: "A Question of Relevance: Re-positioning the Academic Library for the New Information Age" ◆ — Nov 18, 2006 12:47 PM
Join our speakers for a free live webcast on "A Question of Relevance: Re-positioning the Academic Library for the New Information Age" -- a conversation about emerging technology tools and their impact on the role of librarians in the teaching an...
Announcements

Podcast: "Blended Librarians" in the LT Green Room — Nov 9, 2006 11:56 PM
In this episode of the LT Green Room, Susan and Dan are joined by John Shank and Steven Bell, co-founders of http://www.blendedlibrarian.org - a community of librarians who blend instructional design, technology, and librarianship.
Podcasts

Session Recording - "Conversations With Patrons: Extending Your Library's Presence Online" ◆ — Oct 31, 2006 6:21 PM
This talk, "Conversations With Patrons: Extending Your Library's Presence Online", explored the social nature of the web and advocated using social networking sites and student blogs to better understand and assist patrons. A recording is now ava...
Community Session Recordings

FIGURE 8-1
Archived webcasts on the LearningTimes LOC website

phones hooked up to their computers; a virtual whiteboard that allows the speaker and participants to share ideas; a virtual classroom that lets the speaker conduct polls and surveys, lead an Internet tour of websites, and perform desktop sharing (in which participants see on their computers what the presenter is showing on his or hers); and a message board where participants can post questions and interact with other participants.

The BLC strives to offer webcasts on timely topics that are of interest to its membership and are relevant to the field. A sample of some of the recent programming is listed below.

"Tales from a Librarian-Instructional Designer Partnership: Sharing Resources and Knowledge to Support Course Development." When librarians and instructional designers work together, great things can happen. This archive discussed how a librarian and instructional designer at North Carolina State University work together to support graduate-level distance education courses.

"A Look at Newly Emerging Positions at Academic Libraries." This session discussed various new roles for librarians that fit more of the definition of blended librarianship. The guest speakers, Kathryn Shaughnessy and Sean Cordes, spoke about their experiences as librarians in an academic library setting, and the discussion focused on how the role of librarians is evolving.

"Designing Library Experiences for Users with Aradhana Goel of MAYA Design." This session explored how the physical design of the library can affect the way in which users experience the library and the resources it houses.

"Shifting the Balance: Faculty-Led Information Literacy Instruction with William Miller." This archive records a discussion about faculty-led information literacy instruction.

"Powerful PowerPoint: Tips for Ending PowerPointlessness." This is a recording of a discussion led by Kristopher Wiemer on effective uses of PowerPoint for delivering engaging educational presentations.

"Developing Multimedia Teaching and Learning." This is a recording of a discussion about various software programs that allow one to build tutorials, starting with screen capturing and audio recording. The presenters, Sarah Swart, Dan Gall, and Karen Frade, spoke about technical issues, "best practices" for building tutorials and other teaching aids, and assisting faculty with building learning content.

"A Knowledge-Driven Organization in an Information Age." This records a discussion with R. David Lankes about knowledge versus data, the changing role of information, the changing knowledge needs of those seeking library services, and how librarians today can meet those needs.

All of these webcasts are archived within the LearningTimes LOC so that members both past and present can access and view them.

The benefits to participating in a live webcast are that participants can interact with the speaker and other participants. This allows participants to ask questions of clarification as well as share their own perspective or examples at their institutions. The archive does have some benefits as well. While participants are not able to interact with either the speaker or other listeners, they are able to listen to and watch the presentation at their own pace. The archive allows the member to rewind or fast-forward through the presentation so that they can review specific sections and make sure they did not miss important information. Also, at times listeners can experience technical difficulties, and the archive allows members to return to the presentation so they can get any information they might have missed due to such difficulties.

Webcasts offer a number of benefits that traditional face-to-face workshops cannot. These benefits include increased convenience, decreased costs, a self-serve customized environment, and more individualized interactions. The convenience of the live and archive webcasts cannot be overemphasized. The only condition that needs to be met in order to attend a session is to have a computer with an Internet connection. Today most professionals have these technologies both at home and work. Therefore, potential listeners' only primary obstacle to attending on online webcast (besides any possible techno-fear) is another conflicting event or meeting scheduled. It is important to note that while it is possible to multitask during a webcast, we strongly discourage this, because no matter how talented listeners are at multitasking, one's complete attention is diverted from the presentation. If you are planning on multitasking, we recommend only doing so while viewing the archived event should you miss anything, it is easy to rewind.

The fact that you can choose the location from which to join the webcast presentation is a major convenience because it is unnecessary to spend time and energy planning a trip (i.e., travel means, directions, and travel time). This greatly increases the work productivity of participants because they don't have to spend time traveling, which takes them away from their primary work responsibilities. The only time commitment is the time they participate in or watch the archived event.

Another advantage is low costs. Registration for a webcast is often less expensive then a traditional workshop because there are no additional physical facilities that have to be dedicated to a large group. The BLC is fortunate to be able to offer its current programming free of charge because of the generosity of Learning-Times, the guest speakers, and the Blended Librarians Community Advisory Board.

The environment of the webcast can also be advantageous. The advantages of participating in a live or archived webcast include a self-service location and a dedicated terminal. The self-service location means that participants can choose the location that they participate from. Ideally participants should choose a location that provides them with minimal distractions, comfortable conditions (e.g., good climate control, good ergonomics, good lighting, good technical equipment), and ease of access. A dedicated terminal means that unlike participating in a live face-to-face workshop that may have over a hundred attendees and be located in a large room, participants in BLC webcasts can sit directly in front of a computer and adjust the screen and sound level so that they can maximize their ability to hear and see the presentation.

Finally, the increased interactions allow for more engagement between the guest presenter and the participants. As mentioned previously, there are a number of tools associated with the Elluminate virtual classroom; these tools are similar to other web-based collaboration software packages. The tools include a virtual whiteboard and presentation space, an instant message board, a desktop-sharing application, virtual website tour capability, a polling tool, and interactive buttons for clapping, raising your hand, expressing happiness, and expressing sadness. All of these tools can be used to increase the interactions between the speaker and participants. For example, in many BLC webcasts, presenters will do one of the following.

- Have a "voice of the chat" that will keep track of the instant message board and ask the presenter questions that arise
- Include an instant poll to survey the participants
- Make use of the virtual whiteboard or instant messaging to solicit participants' feedback
- Use the virtual website tour tool to take participants to specific websites

Perhaps the biggest advantage to participating in the webcasts is simply that the BLC could not offer these sessions in any other format. There are some challenges associated with webcasts, however. These include lack of face-to-face interaction, technical disruptions, and increased work or home distractions (if participating directly from work or home).

The lack of face-to-face interaction affects webcasts because it can inhibit the informal meeting and gathering of participants after the webcast is concluded. This type of interaction is quite common at library conferences and leads to productive collaborations—a good example being the authors' experience that led to the development of the Blended Librarians Online Learning Community. However, this interaction can occur virtually. For example, the authors never met face-to-face with Hope Kandel before and during the creation of the BLC in the LearningTimes Network.

The increased dependence on advanced Internet communication technologies can also discourage participation in the webcasts. There are a number of reasons for this. First, having the technologies needed for the webcast and feeling comfortable using them are prerequisites. While these technologies are not difficult to use, they are more involved and complex than established technologies such as a telephone. Second, because there are a number of technologies involved, the number of technical difficulties multiplies and can lead to frustrations such as losing a connection with the webcast, losing audio, or losing video.

Finally, the convenience of being able to participate from home or work in the webcasts can also be a detriment if participants are unable to remove distractions from their environment. For example, phone calls, visits from colleagues, and e-mail can serve to interrupt participants during the presentation if they do not isolate themselves from these potential distractions.

Discussion Forums

The BLC has electronic discussion forums available in the LearningTimes LOC (see figure 8-2). These forums allow community members to discuss blended librarian topics. It is common for participants from the BLC webcasts to post discussion topics based on issues that were raised in a previous webcast. This allows members to share and respond to each other and delve into the webcast topics more deeply than can be achieved in a webcast that is sixty minutes long.

There are number of discussion topics, some of which have many responses, while others have relatively few. The following are examples of some of the topics available in the BLC. Discussions related to past webcasts include

- "Shifting the Balance: Faculty-Led Information Literacy Instruction Questions"
- "User-Centered Design in Your Libraries"
- "Is PowerPoint Evil?"
- "Digital Learning Materials Primer"

There are also quite a few discussions that have been posted that are of interest to community members but that are not necessarily directly related to BLC programming. Some of these discussion threads include

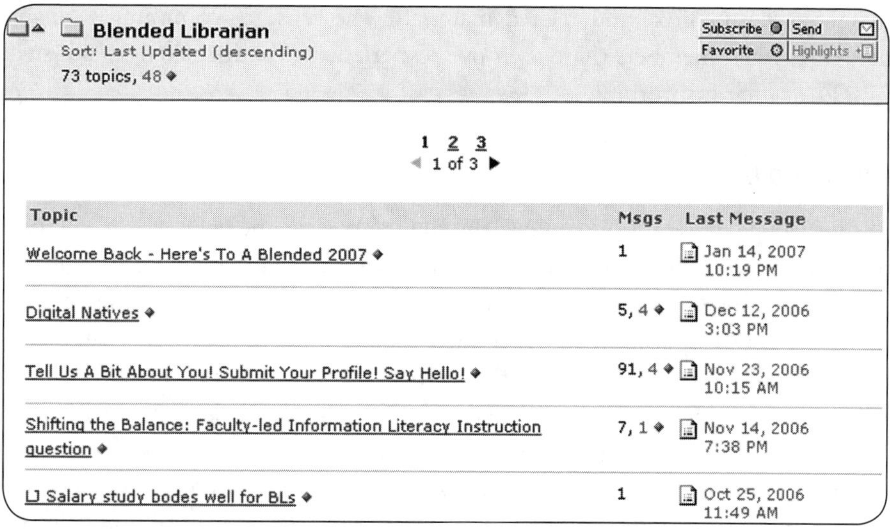

Blended Librarian
Sort: Last Updated (descending)
73 topics, 48 ◆

Subscribe | Send
Favorite | Highlights

1 2 3
1 of 3

Topic	Msgs	Last Message
Welcome Back - Here's To A Blended 2007 ◆	1	Jan 14, 2007 10:19 PM
Digital Natives ◆	5, 4 ◆	Dec 12, 2006 3:03 PM
Tell Us A Bit About You! Submit Your Profile! Say Hello! ◆	91, 4 ◆	Nov 23, 2006 10:15 AM
Shifting the Balance: Faculty-led Information Literacy Instruction question ◆	7, 1 ◆	Nov 14, 2006 7:38 PM
LJ Salary study bodes well for BLs ◆	1	Oct 25, 2006 11:49 AM

FIGURE 8-2
Discussion forums on the LearningTimes LOC website

- "Looking for Colleagues Who Work in Teaching and Learning Centers"
- "Most Youths May Be Tech-Savvy, but They Lack 'Digital Literacy,' Report . . ."
- "Social Learning Technologies"
- "Blackboard Patent News"

Finally, there are discussions that relate to getting more involved in the blended librarians community. Examples of these include

- "Inviting New Members"
- "Looking for a Volunteer"
- "Please Submit Your Profile for the Blended Librarian Workspace"

The discussion forums help develop a deeper sense of community, continue to develop and refine the ideas behind the blended librarian, and allow members to review previous discussion topics. They also help the community to identify possible topics of interest for future webcasts.

The advantage of having a discussion forum is that it gives all members a voice and the opportunity to raise questions and thus to actively participate in developing concepts related to blended librarianship. This is done in an asynchronous environment that allows community members time to think about their responses to posted topic threads. The discussion forums also allow members to share relevant links and related materials. The sense of community can be deepened when members share their own experiences—both challenges and successes—at their institutions.

Online Polls

The LearningTimes LOC also allows the BLC to post online polls. These polls can be useful in building the community and providing feedback to the BLC Advisory Board. The polls provide a simple way for community members to share their thoughts, as well as see how other participants have responded. One example of an online poll is as follows: "In your capacity as a librarian, have you worked with Instructional Designers/Technologists on campus or do you serve as the Instructional Designer/Technologist for your organization?"

The results of this poll show that 43 percent of respondents have worked with an instructional designer or technologist on their campus. Additionally, 33 percent of respondents indicated that they design instructional materials but that they do not consider themselves an instructional designer or technologist. While these polls are unscientific, they can be useful for gaining valuable insight into what the members of the community feel is important and the impact that the BLC is having on its membership. For example, one of the goals of the BLC is to increase the interaction between librarians and instructional designers or technologists. It would be valuable to rerelease the previously discussed poll to see if the current membership would respond with a higher percentage of librarians who have worked with an instructional designer or technologist on their campus.

Online File Cabinet

The online file cabinet functions as the "repository for documents in progress and other information to be reviewed and/or shared" (http://home.learningtimes.net/library/; see figure 8-3). The blended librarian community uses this tool primarily for sharing documents that previous webcast presenters have wanted to share with them. This is useful because it allows both past and future participants in the webcasts to have access to relevant documents.

Resource Lists

The BLC recently took advantage of the resource list tool provided by the LearningTimes LOC and created a Blended Librarian Resource folder. This folder was "created to help the group keep track of useful resources related to design and the Blended Librarian" (http://home.learningtimes.net/library/; see figure 8-4). This

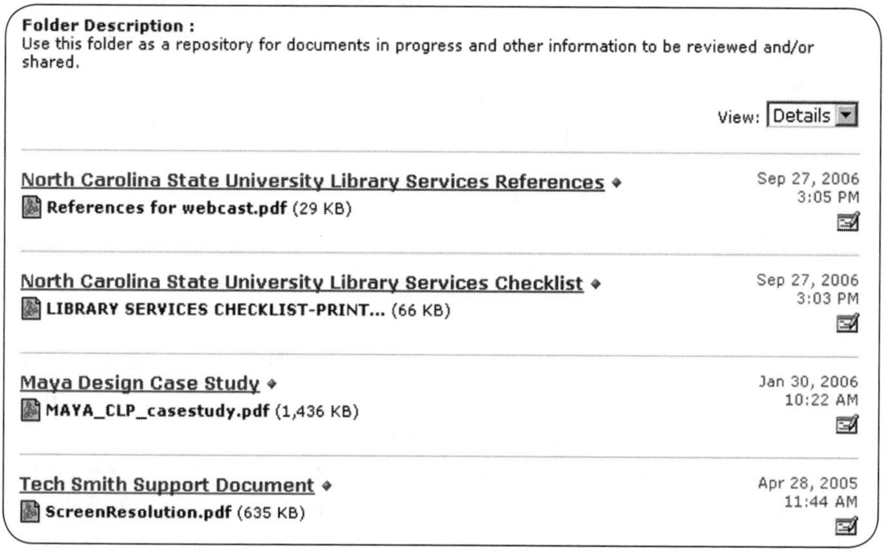

Folder Description :
Use this folder as a repository for documents in progress and other information to be reviewed and/or shared.

View: Details

North Carolina State University Library Services References ◆ — Sep 27, 2006 3:05 PM
References for webcast.pdf (29 KB)

North Carolina State University Library Services Checklist ◆ — Sep 27, 2006 3:03 PM
LIBRARY SERVICES CHECKLIST-PRINT... (66 KB)

Maya Design Case Study ◆ — Jan 30, 2006 10:22 AM
MAYA_CLP_casestudy.pdf (1,436 KB)

Tech Smith Support Document ◆ — Apr 28, 2005 11:44 AM
ScreenResolution.pdf (635 KB)

FIGURE 8-3
Online file cabinet on the LearningTimes LOC website

folder is open to all members to post resources they feel would be relevant and useful. This feature can benefit everyone in the community by tapping the power of communal knowledge. As the membership of the BLC grows, its communal knowledge can also grow, and it benefits everyone to share their knowledge and expertise by posting useful resources.

Instant Messaging and Text Chat

The LearningTimes LOC's chat room is another tool that is available to members of the BLC. This tool allows BLC members to chat with other members or with the larger LearningTimes LOC community. This synchronous communication technology allows members from around the world to communicate in real time and have virtual discussions that can be recorded for archival purposes.

This form of communication is more informal and can take place spontaneously. For example, there is an instant message feature within the LearningTimes LOC that allows all the members logged into the community to see who else is online at the same time. It is possible to instant message a couple of online community members to meet in the chat room and discuss relevant topics.

This tool need not be limited to informal uses only. It can also be used to allow discussions to take place after a BLC webcast has ended. This allows interested members to further discuss the webcast without requiring the presenter to

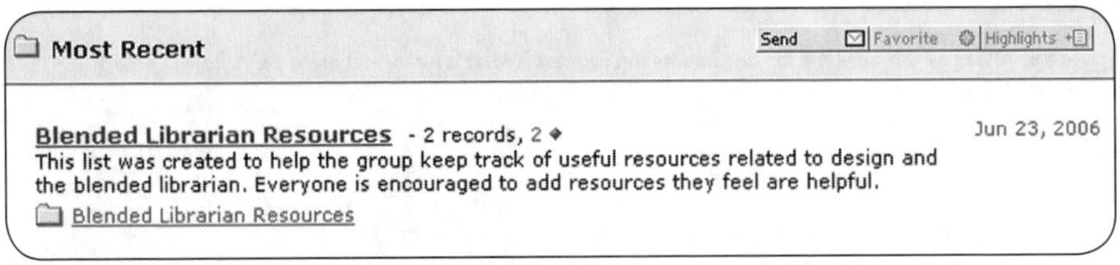

FIGURE 8-4
Resource list on the LearningTimes LOC website

continue with a more formal presentation. This is similar to the time after a traditional face-to-face workshop is concluded and participants move to the front of the room to ask the presenter follow-up questions.

The chat room does have some pitfalls because it is text-based, and the typing skills of the participants can vary widely. If some participants are slow typists or readers, they can have difficulty keeping up with and participating in the chat. Also, if there are a larger number of chat participants, it can become quite confusing if subsets of the participants engage in their own private chats at the same time. These pitfalls aside, the chat room does enhance the communication that can occur within the community.

Virtual Meeting Room

The virtual meeting room is identical to the virtual classroom, the only difference being that it is dedicated to facilitating meetings. The BLC Advisory Board has made use of the virtual meeting room to conduct some of its board meetings. This tool allows members to conduct a virtual board meeting, talk using VoIP, and take meeting notes.

BLC PROFESSIONAL DEVELOPMENT

The authors set out to develop a way for academic librarians anywhere to engage in the development of the blended librarian. Fortunately the BLC was made possible because of technological innovations and LearningTimes' generosity. We realized that besides having a community of people focusing on the blended librarian concepts, it was advantageous to also offer programming that could help librarians, instructors, and staff learn about and develop new knowledge and skills.

The webcasts, as mentioned previously, have numerous advantages in offering a large audience located around the world easy, convenient, and low-cost access to relevant presentations. This type of professional development will not replace traditional face-to-face workshops, but it will become more popular and may someday be a standard part of an employee's professional development training options.

CREATING THE BLENDED LIBRARIAN PORTAL

We decided early on in the development of the BLC that it would be vital to develop a stand-alone website to serve as a portal for blended librarianship. This portal could act as a gateway to the learning community and provide valuable information and resources about it. The blended librarians website, officially known as the Blended Librarian Portal (http://blendedlibrarian.org), offers various types of information, including basic data about the BLC, frequently asked questions, announcements, information on joining the BLC, tools and resources, profiles, video clips, and contact information.

This website allows people to learn more about the BLC without having to join the community. It complements the online community by providing additional resources and information. It also serves as a promotional tool and allows people to see the mission and vision statements of the group. We encourage you to visit this site to learn more about blended librarianship.

JOINING THE BLENDED LIBRARIANS ONLINE LEARNING COMMUNITY

The BLC is a free and open community for all who are interested in joining. It is very easy to join; in addition to following the steps described below, you can learn more about joining by visiting the Blended Librarian Portal. In order to participate in the community and the programming it offers, it is necessary to submit a registration form to the LearningTimes Network. There are three easy steps to accomplishing this.

First, go to the following website: http://home.learningtimes.net/library/.

Second, click on the "join" button and select "option A" and fill out the appropriate information in order to create a new account.

Finally, access to the community will be given and a notice will be sent out upon approval of the new account by LearningTimes.

CONCLUSION

While the BLC is still in the early stages of its growth, that rapid growth demonstrates the appeal of the blended librarian concept and the types of programming and interaction that are provided in the LearningTimes LOC. The BLC is not the only online learning community for librarians. WebJunction is the oldest and largest such community in existence today, with approximately 10,000 members, primarily public librarians. This organization comes out of OCLC and has major donors that contributed to its development and growth. It focuses on providing professional development online workshops, as well as providing resources to help libraries manage their technologies. Additionally, there is the Online Programming for All Libraries (OPAL) organization. This organization is administered by the Alliance Library System, the Mid-Illinois Talking Book Center, and the Illinois State Library Talking Book and Braille Service. It focuses on providing online programming and training for library users and staff.

The difference between the Blended Librarians Online Learning Community and WebJunction or OPAL is that the BLC is the only group that grew from a grassroots movement with no support from an existing library association or organization. This further demonstrates the power of the online learning community as a vehicle to communicate and share new ideas and practices. These online learning communities will continue to grow and mature, and new communities will be formed as communications technology continues to advance and as society becomes more comfortable with online technology. New organizations will arise and existing organizations (e.g., the American Library Association) will adapt to the new paradigms that emerging technologies enable. Librarians of the future will have opportunities like never before to partner and share their successes and challenges. We encourage you to be an active participant in the BLC by going to the website (http://blendedlibrarian.org) to learn more and consider joining your colleagues who are helping to shape the future of the library.

TOPICS FOR FURTHER DISCUSSION

Will online learning communities (e.g., BLC, LearningTimes Network, WebJunction, OPAL) supplant traditional face-to-face workshops as the primary means by which employees get professional development training?

Are there additional ways not mentioned in this chapter that the BLC can assist librarians in professional development?

What are the pros and cons of how the BLC was developed (i.e., grass roots with no funding)?

ADDITIONAL RESOURCES

Bell, Steven. 2005. "Creating Community Online American Libraries." *American Libraries* 36, no. 4 (April): 68–71.

Bell, Steven, and John Shank. 2006. "Conferencing @ Your Computer." *Library Journal* 131, no. 4 (March): 50–52.

9 Evolving through Design Thinking

New Roles for Academic Librarians

> ***We have watched whole professions go out of business as a result of changes in technology. Libraries are not immune. Change must happen soon and across the board if libraries of all types are to remain viable.***
>
> **—David Bishop, university librarian (retired), Northwestern University**

OBJECTIVES

1. Examine three significant societal and technological trends that are changing the way people search and use libraries.
2. Explore how blended librarians will utilize new technologies to shape and define future academic libraries.
3. Identify strategies to make academic libraries more relevant to their user communities.
4. Provide suggestions for steps readers can take to implement and practice design thinking for academic librarianship in their own career and workplace.

INTRODUCTION

The closing years of the first decade of the twenty-first century offer exciting times for academic librarians. Having gone through several years in which both our future viability and the need for our buildings were questioned, our profession has witnessed a renewal in its spirit and practice. Where we once feared threats from search engines, ask-a-question services, and fee-based, online, so-called academic libraries, academic librarians now better understand how to leverage their strengths against the weaknesses of these alternate information services. Still, as a profession, we have a struggle ahead of us. In an environment where our primary user groups can go virtually anywhere to get their information, we will need to work hard at identifying what differentiates the library from its competitors and then capitalize on our strengths. Some of those strengths will involve the types of new knowledge and skills and the overall design thinking mind-set discussed in the preceding chapters. That is why we advocate blended librarianship; it's all about combining a variety of interprofessional skills and new ways of thinking to spur the evolution of the academic librarian.

In this final chapter we will explore some societal and technological trends that are only beginning to affect the ways in which both we and those we serve will search and locate information. As academic librarians we serve the needs of faculty, and as higher education itself evolves, our faculty will increasingly be searching for ways to enhance their teaching and provide students with better learning experiences. We can be there to help them. We also see some exciting new technologies developing, and in many ways they can be thought of as instructional technologies with applications for improved pedagogy. As new generations of students come to our institutions as native users of the latest digital technologies and electronic gadgets, blended librarians must understand those technologies and develop ways to integrate them into our traditional ways of educating students about research methods. It will be an evolutionary period for academic librarians, and we believe that evolution can be shaped by design thinking.

THREE SOCIETAL AND TECHNOLOGICAL TRENDS SHAPING OUR FUTURE

Libraries and the institutions they serve are subject to constant forces of external change. Blended librarians must closely watch, through regular environmental scanning, the larger societal and other trends that shape the future in which our libraries will serve new generations of users. There are three trends in particular that, to our way of thinking, are significant and worthy of our attention. They are already shaping the information search-and-retrieval behavior of our user communities. In the face of the oncoming wave of change, our legacy search-and-retrieval systems' design seems to leave us inadequately resourced and in need of better solutions.

The Simplicity-Complexity Conundrum

By its very nature the research process, particularly at the college level, is inherently complex. It might require the use of resources beyond familiar search engines, such as the library's online catalog or electronic databases. For example, at an institution where I previously worked, the architecture students, early in their academic careers, are assigned two completely different buildings on which to perform a comparative analysis. This might mean comparing a Chinese Buddhist temple and a Romanesque cathedral. Students can easily use search engines to locate images and overviews, but the types of detailed plans, drawings, and commentary needed for a thorough analysis are mostly found in journals, current and past, and books. These students are often perplexed by the assignment and its complexity. To succeed they must learn to navigate databases and other research tools, and as our interactions with them reveal, they are typically unprepared. Furthermore, many can be resistant to managing these more complex research tasks.

This presents enormous challenges for academic librarians as they attempt to introduce some complexity to a group of eighteen- to-twenty-two-year-old patrons—and even adult learners returning to higher education—whose research behaviors are mostly shaped by simple Internet search systems. If their high school instructors were lax about providing research guidelines or establishing what types of articles and how many of them could be used in the preparation of a research paper, then the students are unlikely to adapt well to the complexity they will confront at academic libraries. User education programs, designed appropriately, can encourage students to move from simplicity to complexity. It's possible this line of thinking could be turned on its head to argue that the problem isn't with the students and their threshold for complexity but that it is libraries and their resources that are too complex and that they need to be simplified. No librarian wants to present an unnecessarily complex research system to a user community. We all want our libraries to present minimal or no barriers to access, but the reality is that the nature of research sometimes requires some complexity. As a profession, rather than arguing how things got to be too complex or overwhelming, academic librarians must contemplate how we can use design thinking to establish a manageable balance between simplicity and complexity.

The Age of the User Experience

Though they may present an initial learning curve for individuals, the academic library's research tools can be mastered with some guidance and practice. The challenge for academic libraries is that these are times when both complexity and learning, particularly for electronic information-retrieval systems, are perceived as faults that cause users to go elsewhere. Welcome to the age of the user experience, in which consumers measure the value of products and resources by their simplicity. In this age the expectations for a good user experience are often set by simple search systems such as Google or Yahoo! Academic libraries, unfortunately, are not well equipped to adapt to these new times. With its inherent complexity, the academic library is a poor fit for the age of user experience. We need to adapt our roles so that design thinking plays a greater part in how we create services and offer resources to our user communities. The focus needs to shift to creating a better library user experience.

The age of user experience was, to the best of our knowledge, first discussed by Andreas Pfeiffer in an article titled "Why Features Don't Matter Anymore"

(Pfeiffer 2006). Pfeiffer describes the factors that matter in the age of user experience. Fewer, not more, features are critical; simplicity should rule the user experience, and complexity is a deal breaker; features that go unused only add to complexity. There are other factors, but perhaps the commonality they all share is the element of design. Whether or not any device, digital learning material, or instructional product can provide a good user experience is really dependent on its design. In the age of user experience, the most revered products, such as Apple's iPod or Google's search interface, are widely heralded for their simple designs.

What is often overlooked is that these simple products, while well designed, perform a minimal number of functions. It is much harder to design simplicity into systems that must perform a larger number of more sophisticated functions. The library's online public access catalog (OPAC) is often a target of criticism for a poor design that is too complex for typical library users. That criticism is well deserved to some extent, but a library catalog that serves the needs of everyone from the new freshman to the high-level researcher must have the capacity for complex searching. In the age of user experience, the best products have fewer features that can be used by the majority of the users without extensive training or documentation. Academic librarians, if they can develop a better understanding of design, could be more instrumental in helping the companies that create and market OPACs to develop systems better attuned to the age of user experience. A better OPAC would be just one improvement in creating a far better library user experience. As a profession we need to pay much more attention to any and all resources and services that are "broken" (a popular euphemism for things that deliver a poor user experience) and the ways in which we can use design to fix them.

The Age of Peer Production

Despite its flaws and the controversies it has generated, Wikipedia is an iconic symbol for the age of peer production. It is created by a community of users who add and edit their own content with minimal oversight by authority figures. One of the hallmarks of what is referred to as Web 2.0, a new generation in the development of content on the Web, is that the creation of content is moving from the website owner to the website user. Chris Anderson, editor at *Wired* magazine, wrote an essay in which he described the age of peer production. He wrote: "Now we have an army of amateurs, happy to work for free. Call it the age of peer production. From Amazon.com to MySpace to craigslist, the most successful Web companies are building business models based on user-generated content. This is perhaps the most dramatic manifestation of the second generation Web" (Anderson 2006).

None of this is to suggest that academic libraries should turn their websites into a YouTube or Facebook in which our user communities would create all the content, but this is an important trend, and it may be the right time to begin to design for more user-generated input or content. New resources could be developed to allow this. A library blog is a simple step in this direction. With the proper type of content, it could spur the user community to comment on blog posts or even submit their own blog posts for publication, which is one small way to invite user participation. Of course, it requires a library blog to offer more than just the standard, library announcement–type blog items (e.g., schedule changes, new books, etc.). If a library wants to encourage participation, it must give the users some compelling content that incites them to react or want to share their own ideas. A library could also provide a useful research tool that is based on community content. A good example would be a locally developed bookmarking tool or a personal catalog tool. These types of tools would be based on social community resources such as del.icio.us or Library Thing, where the content is created and shared by users. Some libraries are also experimenting with allowing their user community to add reviews to book records, as Amazon.com does, or allowing them to add "tags" to catalog records the way they can in social bookmark communities like del.icio.us. Wikis are another excellent tool for inviting community participation, and a library could offer a wiki that allows users to build a new type of informational resource that is driven by user content. For example, a new book wiki could allow users to provide their own reviews or recommendations about library books.

Historically, academic libraries are about building communities of social and intellectual exchange within their institutions and offering lectures, displays, and other programs that largely involve or are organized by students and faculty themselves. So in some ways, inviting peer participation at the academic library is perhaps a form of old wine in a new bottle. The difference is that we now have to creatively design systems so that we can extend community participation in our expanding electronic environments. If academic libraries are to prosper in the Web 2.0 world, they will need to rethink and reengineer their ideas about services and resources in order to offer their user communities more opportunity to add, edit, and share content. While we think it is important to follow new Internet trends, because academic librarians need to understand what sites such as YouTube are offering and why its particular form of peer production has made it so successful, we advocate being thoughtful when making decisions about which of these trends to replicate or build upon. Something may work for Amazon.com or Netflix, but the academic library should be careful about jumping on bandwagons to mimic each new trend. Some will make sense for our communities, while others will not. If we approach them with a design thinking mentality, it is more likely we can make good decisions about which ones to develop and implement on the local level.

A BLENDED LIBRARIAN'S RESPONSE

Academic librarianship is clearly faced with some real challenges. The world of information is changing around us, and the pace at which it does so is rapidly accelerating. But the basic core values of academic librarianship have remained steadfast over time. In times of complexity and tumultuous change, returning to those core values and allowing them to guide us can provide individual and organizational stability. As Lee Hisle, then president of the Association of College and Research Libraries, wrote in his landmark editorial on academic library values, "As we lift the veil, clear values will help us face the future" (Hisle 1998). Among the several core values he mentioned was that "we value education as a means to improve life" (Hisle 1998). We advocate the importance of blended librarians integrating both information and instructional technologies into their repertoire of skills, but we do so because integrating them will enable us to evolve in ways that will help us to maintain the core value of education in academic librarianship. From our perspective, as academic librarians, one of the critical functions we perform is supporting the teaching and learning mission of our institutions.

In addition to staying true to the core values of academic librarianship, we also adhere to several core values of blended librarianship:

1. Enhancing libraries' integration into the teaching and learning process
2. Employing design thinking (e.g., BLAAM, A_FLIP)
3. Embracing appropriate instructional technologies
4. Emphasizing community building (i.e., locally and globally)

Partnering and forming learning communities with faculty, instructional designers and technologists, writing experts, professional development staff, and other colleagues enables us to accomplish our number one goal. Similarly, we need to use design thinking in conjunction with appropriate instructional technologies in order to successfully integrate the library more fully into the teaching and learning process at our institutions.

So even as the three types of socio-technological change reshape the environment around us, how we adapt should be guided by our core professional values. Blended librarianship, for many traditionally minded academic librarians, represents a radical role transformation for academic librarianship. But the core value of being committed to promoting education as an individual librarian and a member of the library organization remains unchanged. What is important in times of transformative technological change is the value of being committed to change at a personal level. Blended librarians keep professionally up-to-date so that they are better able to integrate new technologies into their skill set for enhanced pedagogy.

As we write this text there is a new wave of technologies, both driven by and in response to the three socio-technological trends, that offer great possibilities as next-generation instructional technologies. Some of these technologies fall under the umbrella of Web 2.0 and are characterized by their ability to provide better user experiences and more simplified technology tools and to allow for peer production. Blended librarians will better integrate themselves and their services and resources into learning spaces when they are comfortable with these new technologies and are adept at using them as instructional technologies.

In the sections below we provide some examples of Web 2.0 instructional technologies that we believe blended librarians can use to promote the core value of education. We remind the reader that these technologies will change and advance, and that even as this book is being read there are likely to be new and possibly even more exciting instructional technologies on the horizon. It does not matter that some of the technologies we write of today will be superseded by new ones; that is the nature of technology in and beyond the academy. What is important is to retain the core value of being committed to applying whatever the new, perhaps Web 3.0, technologies are to the advancement of the library and its role in the education process. Exploring and mastering new instructional technologies and determining how they fit into the overall design of an improved library user experience is a core value of a blended librarian.

Weblogs

Most of us are familiar with personal and library weblogs (blogs). In the last two years both have expanded exponentially, and there are hundreds of library bloggers and dozens of academic libraries offering their own library blogs. While these types of blogs are useful for disseminating general and personal information, community news, and opinions and commentary, a blended librarian can find other uses for a blog. It could be used to increase the information literacy skills of everyone in the campus community. For example, a blogger could submit posts, including screen shots or video tutorials, detailing techniques to improve research using library databases. A post could also be used to provide links to resources that promote information literacy. These are potentially interesting uses of a blog, but it is difficult to know if any library patrons would actually read these sorts of blog posts. Remember that instructional technology is focused on matching the appropriate technology to enhance teaching and learning. How then might an instructional technologist use blogs to enhance the process?

A library blog developed to support an information literacy initiative would need to be integrated into or developed for specific courses. This would require collaboration with a faculty member so that the information literacy blog would be highly accessible by the students. The blended librarian needs to move the blog from its passivity to a more dynamic tool that is pushed out to the students so that the information it can provide is "where the students are." How can a librarian do that efficiently? As instructional technologists, we also need to be well versed in technologies such as RSS and news aggregators. These Web 2.0 technologies are going to become mainstream over the next decade, and librarians should be developing expertise with them now.

Using another technology referred to as a "feed to HTML converter," instructional technologists have developed a convenient way to move blog posts into any HTML space. That makes it possible to push blog posts into a campus courseware system. It allows students to see the library blog posts whenever they connect to their courseware, and this serves as a good example of truly putting the library's news and information where the students are. Even if they are completely unaware of the library's blog, they will still regularly see the blog posts in their courseware sites. Bell (2005) provides more detail about how this application of Web 2.0 tools works; this article will be of interest to all blended librarians who desire to get more out of their library blog.

Wikis

Wikis are also gaining popularity in higher education as a tool that can facilitate and increase communication by and among students. While a blog project could help to develop a community of learners, a wiki is perhaps even better because it is based on the concept of bringing together a community of learners to develop a single resource that benefits all members through the sharing of information. The unique capacity of a wiki is that it is a form of community writing tool. In other words, each member of the community is able to add new content as well as edit existing content. By now most librarians are familiar with Wikipedia, perhaps the best wiki example and one that demonstrates how a community can develop a shared information resource.

The real question is how a wiki would be used to promote library user education. Are there ways to connect it to learning library resources and promoting effective research skills? A wiki could also be applied to an information literacy assignment. A librarian could create a wiki for a specific course and then add content appropriate to the course and its information literacy outcomes. The wiki could contain objectives for the course's information literacy component and provide details of the assignment created for the course that will help students develop specific information literacy skills. A wiki truly lends itself to a collaborative project, so a librarian using a wiki for an information literacy assignment should develop an activity that would engage the students in gathering information that would be used to collaboratively build an information resource or a joint project. For example, students could develop a group bibliography, or they could develop a resource that other students would use to evaluate websites, or they could develop a group writing activity that would involve an information literacy component.

Currently there are limited examples of wikis being used in information literacy initiatives. That may be because wikis are currently being used primarily for web-based community projects. We suspect that in time more librarians will experiment with this technology as they become more familiar with its attributes and with its capacity to promote collaborative learning. We believe that more collaborative writing tools will become available in a Web 2.0 environment. One such example is Google Docs (http://docs.google.com), which is a collaborative web-based writing resource. Again, the nature of the technology is less important than understanding that as blended librarians we learn and evaluate these technologies and determine in what ways they may fit into our design for a better library and learning experience for our user community.

Personal Response Systems

The personal response system, also known as the "clicker," is a good example of a controversial instructional technology. The clicker device has been the subject of debate in the field of education over whether it contributes to or detracts from learning. As its name implies, the clicker allows individual students to respond to questions from the instructor. The clicker is a small electronic device, with some physical similarities to a remote control unit, that allows students to submit answers to multiple-choice, true-false, or other question types. The questions asked can be factual in nature or they may be opinion oriented. There are a number of publishers and electronics firms that sell the equipment to educational institutions, and most of the products allow faculty to integrate their question slides into existing PowerPoint slide presentations. Instructors, upon giving a question, prompt their students to submit their answers via the clicker. The devices, which work on radio and infrared frequencies, transmit the student responses to the system software, which compiles the responses and summarizes the results for the class.

Those who support the use of clickers claim they are a relatively low-tech method to better engage students in the classroom. Instead of listening passively to a lecture or just taking notes, students are now asked at regular intervals to respond to specific questions about the course content. Clicker critics make the point that the devices are ineffective if what an instructor really wants is to have students more engaged with the course material and with what is happening in the classroom. They claim that students can be completely inattentive to what is happening in class and simply click their responses without really thinking about correct answers. It would be an inappropriate use of an instructional technology if an instructor allowed the technology to create a situation in which he or she is able to evade responsibility for creating a learning environment best suited to the size and needs of the class.

Information literacy instructors should be encouraged to experiment with clicker technology if available at their institution. It can be difficult, especially within a short time frame for instruction, to engage students in a library instruction session. This is especially true when instructing outside of hands-on computing labs. For example, a librarian could ask basic questions, such as "Which of the following is the best synonymous term for . . . ?" and then present several multiple-choice options. This could lead into a discussion about the importance of identifying and using synonymous terms when developing a search strategy. One of the advantages of clicker technology is that it is relatively easy to use. Anyone with the ability to create PowerPoint slides should be able to integrate this instructional technology into their skill set. Personal response systems are the type of instruction technology that blended librarians can use to get students better engaged in library instruction.

Library Aggregator Databases and E-Journals

One overlooked instructional technology that the library profession must do more to promote is the library's own electronic database resources. By some definitions an instructional technology is the hardware, the software, and the systems created for or adapted to an educational purpose. Library aggregator databases and e-journals are certainly systems, their interfaces are a form of software, and they can quite naturally be adapted to education. Almost any library database system, from the big aggregators such as ProQuest, EBSCO, Gale Group, Lexis/Nexis, and Wilson to many niche products, has the potential to help students learn more about specific discipline-based assignments. If information literacy is generally recognized as a valuable skill to learn, for its ability to help students succeed in college and beyond, then offering library databases as tools in learning should certainly qualify them as instructional technologies.

As resources for helping students complete coursework, library databases offer multiple functionalities. First, there is their obvious role as a source of bibliographic and full-text news, information, periodicals, and scholarly content. Second, with the availability of persistent links, they can be integrated into a faculty member's courseware site, which provides the students with direct links to library content. Third, as their technology advances, the databases have added-value features, such as the ability to format citations, that can be used to teach specific information literacy skills.

These are just some examples of the ways in which our library resources can be used as instructional technologies to support teaching and learning. As part of the information literacy initiative, there needs to be ongoing faculty development about using library research databases so that our faculty feel comfortable with these instructional technologies. We should also make sure that our colleagues in the academic technology support areas of the institution are aware of our databases and their features. Given their regular contact with faculty looking for ways to integrate technology into their courses, these colleagues can be our best sales representatives.

STRATEGIES FOR DESIGNING A BETTER LIBRARY EXPERIENCE

These selected instructional technologies offer good examples of the types of tools that blended librarians can adopt as they design methods to integrate the library into the classroom. There are other technologies of equal interest that may be worth further investigation, including podcasting, vodcasting (audio and visual), tablet computers, whiteboards, and other forms of digital video, such as "vlogging," which is video incorporated into a library weblog. These all have distinct possibilities as instructional technologies. As we stated, as these and other new technologies surface, blended librarians need to evaluate them for their potential as tools to promote the use of library services and resources. When appropriate, we need to integrate them in ways that will promote better library experiences for our students and faculty.

But in the turbulent and transformative times we face, just identifying useful technologies will be insufficient to stem the potential tide of marginalization from overwhelming academic libraries. We advocate several strategies that, if appropriately designed, can benefit the future academic library. Some of these strategies are taken from industries that, like academic libraries, are facing competition from the Internet. One such industry is the traditional print newspaper. Others build on strategies that may be more familiar to academic librarians. We offer seven strategies for designing a better library user experience:

- Design for local audiences
- Design for engagement
- Design for personal interests
- Design for information options
- Design for outcomes, not features
- Design to promote success stories
- Design with user education in mind

Design for Local Audiences

Search engines such as Google and Ask.com offer both competition to and cooperation with academic libraries. Cooperative ventures like Google Book Search are mutually beneficial. But academic librarians cannot ignore the fact, as communicated in OCLC's *College Students' Perceptions of Libraries and Information Resources* study (see chapter 4), that the vast majority of students (98 percent) begin their research with Google. We acknowledge there are times when that is the appropriate approach, but search engines are not designed to answer all of the types of vastly different queries people submit. The problem with a search engine is that it attempts to meet all information needs. In attempting to meet everyone's needs, it can sometimes meet no one's needs particularly well. That's where the academic library has a strong advantage. It offers a collection specifically designed to meet the needs of the local community of users. Librarians know the faculty and the students and the information needs of the community. Librarians know the assignments and have experience enabling students to achieve success. Local design is a strategy that many newspaper companies are using to combat Internet competition. They are making a greater effort to focus on local issues because they have an advantage over their virtual competitors in their ability to report local news items and give local citizens a voice in the development of content. We strongly believe that blended librarians need to leverage their local knowledge of their institution's curriculum and assignments to better focus their delivery of information. As discussed in chapter 5, courseware systems offer excellent opportunities to promote the library and integrate it into local learning spaces at both the system and course levels. If we can design courseware-integrated folders that contain just the right databases, links, and assistance that students need to master course skills and assignments, why would they need Internet search engines as their primary research tool? Blended librarians need to develop both the collaborative relationships that give them access to their institution's educational technologies and the knowledge of how these technologies work in order to leverage them for local outreach.

Design for Engagement

A key challenge for all institutions of higher education is to increase student retention and raise graduation rates. It is believed that an important ingredient in encouraging students to stay is to offer them an academically challenging education that truly engages them in the learning process. Students who are underchallenged or bored too often move on to other institutions in search of a better education. The same might be said for students and their research behavior. If academic librarians are unable to provide a research environment and resources that engage and challenge students, they are likely to simply seek out other resources. We often hear that library resources are too complex and cause students to seek out easier resources like search engines. But data from the National Survey of Student Engagement suggests that many college students actually prefer to be intellectually challenged and that presenting challenges, not unreasonable confusion, serves to better engage them. We think that blended librarians can use their instructional design and technology skills to build better learning resources and instructional products that will more effectively engage students in learning how to conduct effective research. These instructional products may take the form of web-based tutorials or exercises embedded in courseware, but to encourage more and better use of the academic library, we will need to better design the resources that engage students in the learning process.

Design for Personal Interests

Not unlike search engines, academic librarians can sometimes suffer from trying to be all things to all members of the campus community, and as a result the library may ultimately serve no one well. Just as we suggested with our discussion of knowing and tapping into local interests, blended librarians can develop resources that offer greater personalization for segments of the user community. Every campus community has resources that cater to the needs of more specialized groups, and it ultimately better serves those individuals and recognizes their personal interests. Academic libraries can seek to offer their resources in a way that makes them more personalized to cohorts within the institution. In the past some academic libraries have offered "my web" options that allow their users to customize the library website to meet their personal preferences. Another option is to develop specialized portals. One advantage the portal has over the personalized web option is that the portal can be designed to promote better research skills. At Philadelphia University the librarians have developed portals that provide examples of designing for personal interests. One portal targets the faculty and students in the business school and offers one-click access to the library's business databases. The portal gathers resources previously spread throughout the traditional library website. The business school portal eliminates confusion and complexity for students trying to find the right resources. We soon developed another portal site for our area studies courses. Nearly all of our students take courses in this track, so we created a portal that brings together on one page a conglomeration of the library's best resources for country news and research. We advocate that blended librarians think in more personalized terms when they use technology such as websites in order to design better research tools and environments for their user communities.

Design for Information Options

Even though search engines can be perceived as competitive forces, academic librarians must acknowledge that they are extremely popular with students; we use them regularly as well. We would be disingenuous professionals to preach to our user communities that search engines are poorly suited to academic research and should therefore be avoided at all costs. It would likewise be unprofessional to suggest that all research should be done only in the library's databases when we know there are types of research for which search engines are better suited. It will only damage our reputations to come off as being all pro-library and anti–search engine. Our users are sophisticated, and they'll recognize quickly that as librarians we are being dishonest with them. As much as we would like to promote the use of our library electronic resources over all nonlibrary resources, it may ultimately be to our advantage to focus more on options and design an options mentality into our resources and user education. We advocate designing for information options, which means to be hospitable to the many different resources to which user communities have access. The goal should be to educate users about all their different information options so that they can select the best ones to resolve their information needs. This will require us to be more open-minded and to help our users better recognize their information needs and then have the ability to match them to the most appropriate resource. In the long run, it will be advantageous to design resources and instructional products that promote information options over those that unrealistically ignore the many options that exist beyond the library's resources.

Design for Outcomes, Not Features

In his article on the age of user experience, Pfeiffer discusses the challenges of too many features. Consider the typical software or electronic devices we all use. Many of them have far more features than we will ever need or use. Adding features, especially when they are unnecessary or poorly designed, simply makes products less satisfying to use. Now consider some of our popular library databases or our library catalogs. Do our users use all the possible features? If not, what features are more impediments to the user than they are benefits? Just as we ourselves never use more than a fraction of the hundreds of features of any typical Microsoft Office software module, the majority of our users likely never use the many features, even some as basic as a field search, in the majority of our databases. The point here is not that we should work to eliminate these features but rather is what we should be emphasizing when it comes to getting our user community to connect with these electronic resources. Our philosophy is that it is better to have a rarely used feature when it is needed than not to have that feature at all. But rather than promoting the many features of our electronic resources that our users are likely to rarely or never need, we should focus instead on just those features that help students achieve learning outcomes. We should focus our instruction sessions about these electronic resources on how they can help achieve learning outcomes. We should go beyond pointing out features to designing instruction sessions and instructional products that connect features to the attainment of institutional learning outcomes. For example, several databases offer features that allow students to create citations in commonly required formats such as MLA or APA. If a stated learning outcome for information literacy is to use information ethically and with proper acknowledgment, then we should focus on how that citation format feature helps the students learn an important skill that is also a learning outcome. We advocate that librarians design with outcomes in mind and focus on them rather than simply identifying large numbers of features that students are just as likely to forget as they are never to need.

Design to Promote Success Stories

Librarians of all types like to talk about Google. Its relationship to libraries could be described as "co-optition," for it is sometimes a cooperative partner and at other times a competitor. Librarians also look to Google for ideas. After all, it's a company that has achieved great things in our own information backyard. Marketers often note that Google grew to be tremendously popular but that it did so without the benefit of major market advertising. Instead, it tapped into new methods of reaching individuals. One of the best-known methods is word-of-mouth advertising. Those who recall the advent of Google will likely remember telling a friend or colleague about this great new search engine or hearing about it from someone else. That's how Google succeeded, by giving those who used it a story to tell others. We believe that library users have many stories to tell that could convey the success they achieve with the help of librarians. So rather than promote services and events, which should be part of the normal routine in any case, we advocate giving the library's users an opportunity to tell their success stories. There are several ways to do this. We further advocate using a form of video that can be integrated into a library blog or a page within the library website. A webcam can be used to capture video, for example, an interview with a successful library user. Software such as videoegg (http://www.videoegg.com) can then be used to upload the video to a blogging site. The goal is to increase use of the library by engaging the library users themselves to promote to others how the library helped them to achieve academic success. Like Google, we must provide our users with stories to share with others so that they can be our partners in getting the community excited about using the library.

Design with User Education in Mind

While we think that all of the aforementioned design initiatives are important, perhaps the one initiative that connects and brings them all together is user education. It doesn't matter how many books, journals, and electronic resources we have, or how great our building is, or how many staff members we have, if the students and faculty don't use any of it. Then it is all just one big institutional waste. As blended librarians we have established that user education is among our highest priorities. One of the blended librarian's core missions is to integrate the library into the teaching and learning process. Without user education, the higher-order accomplishments are all the more difficult to achieve. We believe that evolving through design thinking requires a renewed focus on user education, with an emphasis on designing for user education in many areas in which the academic library functions. Whether it's placing more emphasis on improving the quality of one-on-one instructional situations, integrating the library into the courseware system, or creating a comprehensive information literacy program, we advocate that more and better learning opportunities should be designed into a variety of library activities. The payoff of user education is more than just promoting the better use of library resources. Better-educated library users are more passionate about using the library's services and resources. Users who are passionate about the library are far more likely to seek ways to increase their knowledge and become better researchers. More passionate users are far more likely to let us know what they like and don't like so that we can then design better user experiences for them. Who doesn't want to develop a community of passionate users? We think that the road to get there is built on the foundation of user education.

CONCLUSION

What's next? The answer to that question is up to you, the reader. We hope that this book provides you with the necessary ideas, information, and inspiration to adopt design thinking as a way to reevaluate your future practice of academic librarianship. Making this transformation will be an ongoing process in your career, not an overnight change. We know this because we ourselves are still learning how to be design thinkers, and how to apply these principles to our practice. It takes work and dedication to constantly learn about evolving instructional technologies and how they are being applied in higher education. Achieving collaboration with faculty and fellow academic professionals takes personal sacrifice in both understanding WIIFM and identifying ways to exploit it within your own campus culture. It will be a challenge to find time in your already busy schedule to explore LTAs and DLMs, to experiment with those that others have created, and to possibly develop new ones of your own.

The good news is that if you choose to take the first step on the path to practicing academic librarianship by design, you will not undertake this endeavor on your own. If you have learned nothing else from this book, we hope that you now know that blended librarianship is more than an idea or a set of principles. As you learned in chapter 8, we have designed and developed a learning community that is open to all who desire to learn more about blended librarianship. In the first two years of our community we focused primarily on building instructional technology skills, and many of our webcasts, discussions, and resources reflect the focus on the building of these skills. As we wrote this book, we realized that design thinking can serve as an overarching framework to guide the future growth and direction of blended librarianship. As our community moves into the future, we will be offering more experts and discussions on topics related to design thinking and how it can be applied practically in library settings.

Just as design thinkers are described as "hybrid professionals" (Hempel and McConnon 2006) because they combine multiple disciplinary skills (e.g., design, marketing, information technology, ethnography, etc.) into a single mind-set, we believe that blended librarians are the hybrid library professionals of the future.

Already we have seen an increase in the number of professional positions being advertised by academic libraries that require a blending of instructional design and instructional technology skills. We believe that just as fields such as business and engineering recognize the importance of design thinking for innovation and creativity, its value will be recognized in our profession as well. We anticipate that it is only a matter of time before design thinking appears in academic library job descriptions along with traditional candidate qualities such as being dynamic, creative, innovative, and forward thinking. From our point of view, design thinkers demonstrate all those qualities.

While we've advocated many changes to the traditional role of academic librarians and acknowledge that change is hard, we recognize the importance of maintaining the core values of academic librarianship as expressed by Hisle, as well as the core values of blended librarianship as we described them in chapter 1. We know that our profession and the tools and resources we use are destined for dramatic change. If we recognize our core values and allow them to guide us as we confront the turbulent future, we will maintain a course that is always focused on achieving our primary outcomes. So if you think of the transformation to academic librarianship by design as a journey, like all of them it begins with a single step. Unlike many, there is already a community that welcomes you and will be there to support you along the way. We hope you will join us there.

TOPICS FOR FURTHER DISCUSSION

In addition to the three socio-technological trends discussed in this chapter, what other important trends do you think are ones to which academic librarians should be paying attention?

In what ways have you been using instructional technologies to either support existing library services, develop new ones, or support faculty in the teaching and learning process?

In what ways could the Blended Librarians Online Learning Community help you learn more about design thinking, blended librarianship, or any of the other topics discussed in this book?

What are some specific things you could do in your library to design a better experience for your users?

References

Albanese, Andrew Richard. 2003. "The Top Seven Academic Library Issues." *Library Journal* 128 (March 15): 43.

Anderson, Chris. 2006. "People Power." *Wired* 14 (July): 132.

Bell, Steven J. 2003. "A Passion for Academic Librarianship: Find It, Keep It, Sustain It—A Reflective Inquiry." *Portal: Libraries and the Academy* 3, no. 4: 633–42.

———. 2004. "Promotion through 'Teachnology': Using LTAs (Low Threshold Applications) to Collaborate with Faculty." *NetConnect* (Winter): 15–16.

———. 2005. "Where the Readers Are." *NetConnect* (Fall): 8–13. http://www.libraryjournal.com/article/CA6269278.html.

Bell, Steven J., and John Shank. 2004. "The Blended Librarian: A Blueprint for Redefining the Teaching and Learning Role of Academic Librarians." *College and Research Libraries News* 65, no. 7 (July/August): 372–75.

Brown, Tim. 2005. "Strategy by Design." *Fast Company* 95 (June): 52–54.

Chickering, A. W., and S. C. Ehrmann. 1996. "Implementing the Seven Principles: Technology as Lever." *AAHE Bulletin* 49, no. 2: 3–6.

Chickering, A. W., and Z. F. Gamson. 1987. "Seven Principles for Good Practice in Undergraduate Education." *AAHE Bulletin* 39, no. 7: 3–7.

Christiansen, Lars, Mindy Stombler, and Lyn Thaxton. 2004. "A Report on Librarian-Faculty Relations from a Sociological Perspective." *Journal of Academic Librarianship* 30 (March): 116–21.

Cohen, David. 2002. "Course-Management Software: Where's the Library?" *EDUCAUSE Review* 37 (May/June): 12.

DeBlois, Peter B. 2005. "Leadership in Instructional Technology and Design: An Interview." *EDUCAUSE Quarterly* 28, no. 4: 12–17.

Dempsey, Beth. 2005. "Power Users." *Library Journal* 130 (December 15): 72–75. http://www.libraryjournal.com/article/CA6289901.html.

DeRosa, Cathy, et al. 2006. *College Students' Perceptions of Libraries and Information Resources.* Dublin, Ohio: OCLC.

DeSieno, R. 1995. "Netlaw: The Faculty and Digital Technology." *Educom Review* 30, no. 4: 46–48.

Farson, Richard. 2005. "Management by Design." http://www.wbsi.org/farson/com_mgtbydesignr.htm.

Hawkins, Brian L. 2001. "Information Access in the Digital Era." *EDUCAUSE Review* 36, no. 5: 50.

Hempel, Jessi, and Aili McConnon. 2006. "The Talent Hunt." *Business Week* 4004 (October 9): 66–72.

Heskett, John. 2002. *Toothpicks and Logos: Design in Everyday Life.* Oxford: Oxford University Press.

Hisle, Lee. 1998. "Facing the New Millennium: Values for the Electronic Information Age." *College and Research Libraries News* 59, no. 1 (January): 6–9. http://www.ala.org/ala/acrl/acrlpubs/crljournal/backissues1998b/january98/candrljanuary1998.htm.

———. 2002. "Top Issues Facing Academic Libraries: A Report of the Focus on the Future Task Force." *College and Research Libraries News* 63, no. 10 (November).

Jeffries, Shellie. 2000. "The Librarian as Networker: Setting the Standard for Higher Education." In *The Collaborative Imperative: Librarians and Faculty Working Together in the Information Universe,* ed. Dick Raspa and Dane Ward, 120–21. Chicago: American Library Association.

Kelley, Tom, and Jonathan Littman. 2001. *The Art of Innovation: Lessons in Creativity from IDEO, America's Leading Design Firm.* New York: Currency Books.

Kotler, Philip, and G. Alexander Rath. 1984. "Design: A Powerful but Neglected Strategic Tool." *Journal of Business Strategy* 5 (Fall): 16–21.

LearningTimes Library Online Community. http://home.learningtimes.net/library/.

Long, Sarah A. 2006. "Ever-Changing Landscape Adds New Dimension for Librarians." *Daily Herald,* August 13. http://www.sarahlong.org/ourlibraries/read/index.php?articleID=271.

Merritt, Jennifer, and Louis Lavelle. 2005. "Tomorrow's B-School? It Might B a D-School." *Business Week* 3945 (August 1): 80–81.

Morgan, Glenda. 2003. "Faculty Use of Course Management Systems." *ECAR Key Findings,* May. http://www.educause.edu/ir/library/pdf/ERS0302/ekf0302.pdf.

Pfeiffer, A. 2006. "Why Features Don't Matter Anymore." *E-Week,* January 23. http://www.eweek.com/article2/0,1895,1914493,00.asp.

Potter, Norman. 2002. *What Is a Designer: Things, Places, Messages.* London: Hyphen.

Raspa, Dick, and Dane Ward, eds. 2000. *The Collaborative Imperative: Librarians and Faculty Working Together in the Information Universe.* Chicago: American Library Association.

Reingold, Jennifer. 2003. "Still Angry after All These Years." *Fast Company* 75 (October): 89. http://www.fastcompany.com/magazine/75/angry.html.

Richlin, L., and M. D. Cox. 2004. "Developing Scholarly Teaching and the Scholarship of Teaching and Learning through Faculty Learning Communities." *New Directions for Teaching and Learning* 97: 127–35.

Seels, Barbara, and Zita Glasgow. 1998. *Making Instructional Design Decisions.* 2nd ed. Columbus, Ohio: Prentice-Hall.

Shank, John D. 2003. "The Emergence of Learning Objects: The Reference Librarian's Role." *Research Strategies* 19, nos. 3/4: 194.

Shank, John, and Steven Bell. 2006. "A_FLIP to Courseware: A Strategic Alliance for Improving Student Learning Outcomes." *Innovate* 2, no. 4 (April/May). http://www.innovateonline.info/index.php?view=article&id=46.

Walter, Scott. 2000. "Case Studies in Collaboration: Lessons from Five Exemplary Programs." In *The Collaborative Imperative: Librarians and Faculty Working Together in the Information Universe,* ed. Dick Raspa and Dane Ward, 40–41. Chicago: American Library Association.

Warger, T. 2003. "Calling All Course Management Systems." *University Business* 6, no. 7 (July): 64–65.

Index

Y

Steven J. Bell is Associate University Librarian for Research and Instructional Services at Temple University. Previously, he was Director of the Paul J. Gutman Library at Philadelphia University. Earlier in his career, he was Assistant Director of the library at the Wharton School of Business at the University of Pennsylvania, where he also earned his Ed.D. in 1997. He writes and speaks frequently on topics such as information retrieval, library and learning technologies, and academic librarianship. An adjunct professor at Drexel University's College of Information Science and Technology, he teaches courses in online searching and academic librarianship there. He maintains a website, Steven Bell's Keeping Up Web Site, and a weblog, *The Kept-Up Academic Librarian*, that promote current awareness skills and resources. He is a cofounder of the Blended Librarians Online Learning Community on the LearningTimes Network. For additional information about the author and to find links to the various websites he publishes and maintains, point your browser to http://stevenbell.info.

John D. Shank has been in the field of higher education since 1996. He received his master's degree from Drexel University's College of Information Science and Technology. Since entering the field he has worked in various capacities at several academic institutions, including Montgomery County Community College, Haverford College, and Bryn Mawr College. Currently he is the Instructional Design Librarian and the Director of the Center for Learning Technologies at the Berks campus of Pennsylvania State University. He has presented hundreds of faculty development workshops, lectures, and seminars at various universities and colleges and given presentations at regional and national conferences. Shank has also authored and coauthored articles and book chapters on the topic of integrating instructional technology into library services. He is a cofounder, along with Steven Bell, of the Blended Librarians Online Learning Community.